trials

&

tribalations

~::~

a menagerie of aesthetic
arrangements

~::~

trials
&
tribalations

-::- a menagerie of aesthetic arrangements -::-

by

iowan tribal

BellyFeast Publishing
New York

Published by **BellyFeast Publishing**
bellyfeast@yahoo.com

Copyright © 2007 **iowan tribal**
Forewords Copyright © 2007 **Shelley Nicole Jefferson** & **Christopher A. Smith**
Nut & Geb artwork (pg 93): **Entrfied Ka Ptah**
Book Layout Design,
Cover Art, Editing &
BellyFeast Logo: **iowan tribal**

ISBN: 978-0-6151-5802-0

Words of Honor...

these poems, free verses, streams of consciousness, thoughts and prose that span from 1992 to 2007 and beyond are dedicated to those who are still searching for the strength to let their spirits shine like they deserve to. may you all find that strength in these words that i share with you.

my journey

is

your journey

is

our collective journey.

In Appreciation Of...

:: The Creator :: Ntr Hru Maát (My Sun-ManChild in the Promised Land) :: The Tribble Fam (Mom [rest in peace] / Dad / Bruce / John) :: Aunt Rose [rest in peace] :: Aunt Diane :: Aunt Marion :: Aunt Brenda :: Uncle Harold :: Lorraine & Bill McCloud :: Karìm McCloud :: Black Lotus – Shelley Nicole Jefferson / Jackie Harris / Kimmi Knox /Vilma Alvarez / Mechelle Rayford-Hutch & Ellehcem Hutchinson :: Christopher Smith :: Ian Friday :: Robert Stone-Flowers :: Alafia Brown :: Ubiquita NYC :: The Unscene (Jamyla & Pierre Bennu) :: Ti Randall :: Sylvia V. Hillman :: Louis Reyes Rivera :: Cherise & Stephen Trahan-Miller & The entire Ashay Fam :: Entrfied Ka Ptah & Khaleedah Ishe & Elahi Shai Yemanja :: Malikka & Ozziah Phillips :: Regina Brooks :: Laura Williams :: Joi Harvey :: Vonetta Booker-Brown :: Beluvid Ola Jendai & Melanation :: Derick Cross :: Anisa Fujah :: Alice & Alicia Crowe :: Julia "JayGeeOh!" O'Farrow :: Emily "Flying Mermaid" Fisher :: Ronald Lavender :: Ed Toney :: AJ Wone & da Binaries & Keedah O.G. Giannetti :: Mabili Kregg Ajamu :: Casa Atabex Aché :: SupaNova SLOM :: Sonshu Hitohana Inu & Sonic Boom :: From back in da dayz: The Tea Party, The Medicine Show Theater, The Crash House, Thought Forums, Brooklyn Moon, Yr Teop, The Point & The African Poetry Theater :: And most of all, Frantz "Pep" Simpson... (rest in peace, bro.) ::

✳iowan tribal

the setup from the yoni

For: Word

As humans we have a tendency to set artists apart by gender or race. While thinking this gesture of showering people with accolades by setting them atop of their particular group is flattering, I think it is really just separating them from some of the great people that they should be linked to. With that in mind I am not going to compare Iowan Tribal with any other poet. I am just going to emphatically state that she is one of our greatest writers. There is no need to pull her apart or set her into a category. Like Nina she will put a spell on you that will trigger your senses and fill your center.

I met Yolanda Tribble in a space and time like no other. Sometimes when I think back on the divine timing of that gathering of spirits, it feels like an excerpt out of a fairytale. For Yolanda it was a time of Mohawks, big knives, huge crushes, crazy boyfriends, beautiful women and young pens. Underneath her *"Watch yourself cuz I'll kick your ass"* exterior, stood a beautiful woman with words bursting from her hands. Like the lotus, I watched Yolanda bloom into Iowan Tribal and rise from the mire.

Shortly after meeting Iowan, she told me she was reading her poetry in the City [Manhattan]. Around the same time I was divinely guided to the Promised Land or some might call it Mecca. I'm talking about Brooklyn and the Tea Party to be exact. Sundays would never be the same. Iowan didn't start writing there, but that is where it grew into many of the pieces you will read on these pages. We were at the epicenter of a movement like no other.

Yolanda had already unleashed the *impact of her grill* on Manhattan, but in Brooklyn Iowan would befriend a *mad roach*, find her *front porch rhythm* and *honor her TaTa's* like a bard with an axe to grind. Only Iowan can make pussy sound good, even when being cussed out about disrespecting it.

Iowan is not just a writer she is a visionary. From her pen a Black Lotus bloomed and she blessed me with a petal of own. Three women would eventually become six and I became part of her tribe of warrior women that would become legends in our own time. We joined forces as a way to express ourselves, but through comedy and spoken word wound up collectively healing in the process. Our *Tales from the Tit-T* was the precursor to the *Vagina Monologues*. Black Lotus pulled no punches. Who else would have the nerve to produce *Spermicide Puppet Theatre*? We were bold, honest and told stories of the good, the band and the gruesome that shaped and changed our lives. Black Lotus was more than a group it was our creative elixir, and if left to Iowan it will bloom again.

In a song written by a good friend, there is a line that says, "Don't mess with singers cuz you might end up in a song." Well the same is true of poets. They say the pen is mightier than the sword, but in the case of Iowan you better watch out for both. At this very moment she is learning that I call her the Goddess of Get Back! If you cross her line or the line of anyone she loves you are sure to be at the tip of her pen. Don't worry, she won't say your name directly, but be clear that she has no problem "callin' muthafuckas out!" But that is only one side of this multifaceted author. She has the ability to transport you through time with her rhymes. Outer space is no match for her inner. Iowan has the capacity to love you so hard that you can't help but hold on and beg for more. She will make you moan the writer's lament of "Damn! I wish I had written that!"

Iowan found so much love in the Brooklyn arts community that she had no choice, but to flourish. From solo to Black Lotus to the Woman of Bogalon to the Tea Party Collective to being a mama and back to solo. Iowan is as brilliant as the stars.

The woman who has grown into Iowan is Yo to me. She is my friend, my sister and my reflection. We are kindred spirits. In a time when I had no idea how my life would turn, she appeared with a smile full of teeth and a heart full of warmth. We both looked to each other for clarity and understanding of the life we were creating and the people we were drawing into our circle. We have broken bread, shared laughs and shed tears together. I watched her give birth to sun and I haven't been the same since. In the words of the great poet Heavy D, "I got nuttin' but love" for this woman. More love than these pages can hold. More love than my heart can handle.

Shelley Nicole Jefferson
www.blakbushe.com
www.myspace.com/blakbushe
info@blakbushe.com
Brooklyn, New York
2007

the set up from the lingam

So I'm writing this introduction with a theme song I felt would be most appropriate for the soulful literary journey that you've just committed yourself to, dear reader. What song, you may ask? "Theme From Cleopatra Jones" by Joe Johnson. Let me break it down for you. The words you're about to read, fall in love with, incorporate into your daily existence to major and minor degrees are just a piece of who Iowan Tribal really is. Allow me to explain further.

Iowan is first and foremost a strong, deeply beautiful Black woman. A soul sister in a time when we almost forgot what that meant. Iowan is a deeply loving and devoted mother to a wonderfully spirited manchild who I am honored to call my godson. She's an artist in the same venerable sense we hold the griots of Mother Africa in. The same regard we hold Ella, Aretha, Nina and Mahalia in. Most of all, to me, she has been a trusted sister, a loyal friend and an exquisite soul to be around. If I am lucky enough to have daughters in my lifetime, I have always felt that I would want them to have the same indomitable spirit that Iowan possesses. I've been extremely blessed to bear witness to such a spirit that has manifested itself in her work. Imagine that in person times ten.

So, dear reader, bear witness to that powerful spirit as you read these offerings of wisdom, light, joy, pain and ultimately love. And then you'll feel as blessed as I have been.

Peace, Love and Respect,
Christopher A. Smith
aka **infinitewords**
infinitewords@yahoo.com
www.myspace.com/crossislandstateofmind
Cambria Heights, New York
2007

the arrangements

verse 1

-:::~

the abode of the heart

what are the things that are most precious to me? what are the instances that reinforce the innocence within me that keeps me from being defeated by cruelty and carelessness? how have i protected that special part of myself so that the light within me shines no matter what adversity i am faced with?

these are the conditions that have birthed these 10 pieces in this verse 1. in my daily grind to be a productive and responsible adult, there are times when i need to tap into my inner innocence so that i will not be forced to look at the world through constant jaded eyes.

i have created this safe place within me that is untouchable by interlopers and perpetrators. a cocoon of warmth that reinforces that there is more good in the world than bad...

Mother, thy name is Greta.
You, a full, voluptuous brown skinned woman.
A woman who was my mother on this earth,
From whom I exited from thy womb,
Passing through thy womanhood,
With thy thick brown thighs as my landscape.
Held by all to see,
I was wrapped and held by thee
And with thy breasts, you nourished me.
From the moment of conception,
I loved thee deeply.

Mother, thy name is Greta.
You were my brothers' and my Defender
As we traveled through childhood.
You tried your best to do good
The only way you knew how.
A beautiful black diamond
That was flawed,
You fought for us tooth and claw.
Through thy ebony eyes I saw
Strength,
Pride,
Stubbornness,
Pain.
But from the moment of conception,
I loved thee deeply.

Mother, thy name is Greta.
My worst enemy and my best friend.
We fought like jungle cats
And we loved like sisters as we sat
At the kitchen table when we chat
About how you yearned to be free
From thy own mother's yoke.
But the sins of the mother
Becomes the sins of the next mother.
A vicious cycle: over and over.
A problem never truly recognized,
Therefore never truly solved
But from the moment of conception,
I loved thee deeply.

Mother, thy name is Greta.
Thou art my template
To break the vicious cycle of hate
That was taught in ignorance.
I will use thy loving nature
As a guide for a better future
For thy generations to come.
I will use thy pain and anger
As a lesson to be learned
For thy generations to come.
For thou art my example of a beautiful
Black Woman
Even as a black diamond flawed
Because from the moment of conception,
I loved thee deeply.
In Loving Memory,

Your Daughter
~ :: ~

5

front porch rhythm

i felt a gentle but firm tug of my hair and instantly i complied, leaning back into the warmth of her chocolate brown thighs as we sat out on the stoop.
i sat one step lower than hers and i closed my eyes and sighed.
i felt the softness of her thighs and smelled the scent of the vaseline that she had rubbed into them earlier.
like a surgeon precise with a scalpel, she started at the center of my hairline and parted backwards from my forehead.
though her hands were thick and nearly the size of my daddy's, she never dug into my scalp.
she parted with her right hand, as she held my bushy mane down with her left.
never once did she had to do a part over...
like i said, she was precise.
while cracking her gum vigorously, she would gather up the left side of my hair, and with one of those rubber bands she would collect from around the house, put a big fat puff of hair on that side.
then she would begin sectioning my right side and commenced with the braiding.
there was a rainbow array of barrettes that she had picked out, sitting in a pile next to her.
see, she had plans for my head, regardless of what i thought... but it didn't matter because this was one of many moments when i could relish the closeness of her.
i was so content that i would be 1/2 asleep as she worked the magic of her nimble fingers... weaving the spells of satisfaction, closeness and warmth, placing me in a state of trance.
with her at the helm of my crown, i could relax and have some reassurance as a child that life was filled with blue jays, monarch butterflies, steel pan drums and ramsey lewis.
blue magic, sulfur 8, royal crown, bergamont, dax, dixie peach and sometimes good ol' vaseline.
now, them was some the greases that she would dip into to get a glob on her right index fingertip and oil my scalp with.

part (goes the comb)
dip, dab (goes the finger from jar to scalp)
rub, rub (goes the greasing)
braid braid braid (her hands weaved)
snap (goes the barrette)

this was her rhythm that she played on my head and in my hair.
a natural rhythm.
the rhythm from mother to daughter.
this was the eternal rhythm that all black mothers passed on to their black daughters.
from the motherland to the world.
sitting on front porches in the summertime - butterflies & bees, birds & trees, flowers & breezes, barking dogs & grass that's green, & of course children playing in the streets.

6

part (goes the comb)
dip, dab (goes the finger from jar to scalp)
rub, rub (goes the greasing)
braid braid braid (her hands weaved)
snap (goes the barrette)

the eternal rhythm.
so i sit there between my mother's thighs, eyes shut, being lulled by the sharing of
closeness, love and ancestral memories of motherland rhythms.
you see, my mother and i... we connected on a higher, spiritual level.
she gave important, secret messages and i received them subtly to pass on to my own
in the future.
it was like the electrical information would travel from her brain, down through her
neck, gathering into her chest cavity, to be sent in equal amounts down her forearms.
destination: her fingertips...
to be dispersed into the strands of my hair and straight to the brain.
and i knew... i knew...
i knew that when i have my daughter one day, we will also share the closeness of
that eternal rhythm. the rhythm of:

part (goes the comb)
dip, dab (goes the finger from jar to scalp)
rub, rub (goes the greasing)
braid braid braid (her hands weaved)
snap (goes the barrette)

see, it was from my mother's seed that i sprung.
and though she could not teach me everything, she taught me more than she could
ever realize when she had passed to me the eternal rhythm.
a non-verbal legacy.
it was more valuable than gold and more precious than diamonds.
it was a gift that once given, could never be taken away.
it was more than just my own memories.
it was collective and ancestral and spiritual and timeless.
it was real.
so listen...

part (goes the comb)
dip, dab (goes the finger from jar to scalp)
rub, rub (goes the greasing)
braid braid braid (her hands weaved)
snap (goes the barrette)
[a dog barks]

part (goes the comb)
dip, dab (goes the finger from jar to scalp)
rub, rub (goes the greasing)
braid braid braid (her hands weaved)
snap (goes the barrette)
[a child laughs]

part (goes the comb)
dip, dab (goes the finger from jar to scalp)
rub, rub (goes the greasing)
braid braid braid (her hands weaved)
snap (goes the barrette)
[a cardinal sings]

part (goes the comb)
dip, dab (goes the finger from jar to scalp)
rub, rub (goes the greasing)
braid braid braid (her hands weaved)
snap (goes the barrette)
[and a child sleeps, lulled by the warmth of her mother's chocolate brown thighs]

~ :: ~

brooklyn

chain linked fences and train yards
shooting craps and playing cards
hazy jazz and tall windows
afro-beats and funky flows
high ceilings... suspended fans
cops that just don't give a damn
tree roots pushing through concrete
parking tickets... busy streets
bodegas and old winos
brooklyn people gotta pose
hats with pop and lots of locks
hanging out up on the block
bus exhaust and screeching brakes
old brownstones and more keepsakes
block parties and barbecues
muddy waters doing blues
concrete jungle for street kids
ex-cons out from doing bids
stop to chat with old man Nat
who tell young cats where it's at
sun kissed people on a stroll
house music and bodies roll
be-bop hip-hop finger pops
brooklyn's sounds that never stops...

~:~

a partridge in a pear tree

& i spin around
      & around
      & around
      & around...

i see azure sky &
      green grass &
         brown bark of tree &
            pale green pears &
               fiery orange & yellow tiger lilies &
                  scarlet poinsettias &
                    snowy daisies with canary yellow centers.
a harmonious
      symphonic
         orchestra
            of
               flora
                  coloratura
                    With Nature's Mother
                       as the maestro.
as i spin faster & faster,
      my patchwork dress
         that mama made me
            swirls in the wind
               like a cloth windmill
                  & my eyes see
                    Nature's colors swirling
                    like crazy mad tie-dyes
                      & psychedelica.

i teeter & i totter & i fall
      ever so gently
         & on my forehead
            alights a partridge
               who looks down at me
                  from her vantage
                    into my eyes
                      & tells me about love
                      without the hindrance
                       of words.

~ :: ~

forsythia

~ i ~

white patent leather shoes
faintly scuffed on the sides
feet done grew some
so forsythia walked
pigeon-toed
to ease her discomfort
on the way down yonder
from church
to grandmama's house
for some fried chicken
and collard greens
she never cared too much
for rice
took up good space
from them other fixins
she was fixin to get

~ ii ~

louisiana sun beat down
like tom-tom drums
white collar stained dingy
mama done worked hard
pressin that head
this mornin
but her sunday curls
lost their battle
in this here heat
dixie peach and sweat
sloppy lovers minglin
at the nape of her neck
she longed for
pigtails and jeans
wit holes in the knees
that way
she ain't gotta act
so dang prissy
tomboy, tried and true
she be climbin fig trees
racin her bike down dirt streets
and runnin through cane fields
like her britches were on fire

~ iii ~

but one day outta the week
she gotta set her Self aside
and endure the day long
"goin to hell" sermons
from pastor
dabbin his thick dark brow
wit a starched white kerchief
as he worked up his lather
brimstone and hellfire and damnation
all he preached
no chance of redemption
so she gazed
longingly
over to her right
out a half opened
stained glass window
Self emancipation
only time she understood salvation
only time she felt closest to christ

~ iv ~

forsythia walked thru
the screen door
relieved to see
grandmama
wit a mess a greens simmerin
in a blackened pot
on a wood burnin stove
droppin in bits of
smoked ham and chopped onions
grated garlic and tomatoes chunks
grandmama cookin
creatin
servin up recipes
wit equal measures
of indulgence and discipline
a dash of yes
and heapin spoonfuls of no
one hand stirrin and
the other moppin her unlined face
wit a dish rag

older than the pot and the stove
blisterin hot summer days
don't stop dis kinda woman
from her sunday ritual

~ v ~
married at 14
she lived passed two husbands
and bore eleven chirren
cleaned houses
for them white folks
durin the week
pressed hair
for black folk
on the weekends
lived through
wars and depressions
that plagued her life
survivin harshness
this strong willed woman
was burnt and hardened
around her heart edges
ain't a damn thing
a man can do for her
that she can't do for herself
probably why most times
forsythia feared her
more than loved her

~ vi ~
grandmama always say
she her special grandbaby
always mindin her manners
whenever she came on over
after sunday church
but that girl saw what
grandmama's switch can do
and her aim's way too tight
when a shoe is thrown
dang near put your eye out
if you ain't
quick enough to duck
her cousins who live

wit this old southern woman
always suffered
her quick tempered wrath
and heavy hand
harder the head
softer the behind
so forsythia stayed way below
grandmama's radar

~ vii ~
liniment and amber
saturated her nostrils
when she reached up
on tippy toes and
gave grandmama a kiss
on her soft, fuzzy cheek
findin a stool nearby
she sat
and watched
and learned
as the older woman
prepared to fry up
freshly killed chicken
she caught
from her hen yard
feathers plucked
by her hands
same hands reachin
for used fry grease
kept in an old crisco can
on the kitchen table
forsythia's mouth
watered shamelessly

~ viii ~
her cousins' sounds
playin outside
frolickin imps
runnin and stompin
in this dang heat
tempted forsythia but
grandmama's cookin
held her fast

besides no tellin what
her fool cousins
were gettin into
end up havin that woman
shakin down trees for
a good piece of switch
to get a bad piece of behind

~ ix ~
no surprise
the cousins
messin around throwin
dirt-bombs at each other
end up shatterin glass
all over the kitchen floor
faces ashy from all that dang dust
they done kicked up runnin around
now tear streaked from cryin
cuz grandmama done
tap their little behinds
then made their rusty butts
go on down to the well
bring back some water
to scrub floors on hands and knees
for punishment
and whenever
grandmama's back was turned
they blessed forsythia
wit cuttin eyes
while she sat there at the table
still in her sunday clothes
and slightly scuffed
white patent leather shoes
tearin up some
collard greens and chicken

~ x ~
grandmama in her rocker
movin to and fro
shaded from late afternoon sun
on the rickety porch
sewin patchwork
now in t-shirt

and torn faded jeans
and pigtails
forsythia climbed
a young cypress tree
in the front yard
wit wooden planks
already nailed in its scaly bark
the louisiana sun
that grandmama hid from
jus loved all over
that girl's brown skin
gleamin like polished bronze
tomboy, tried and true
splendid, none the less

~ xi ~
grandmama called her
down from the tree
took her by the hand
and led her to the side
of the old farm house
where the sun shone brightest
she showed the girl
her namesake
them wild bushes wit
bright yellow flowers
bloomin along the length
of thin long branches

forsythia
grandmama smiled
her favorite grandbaby
her forsythia
and the girl wrapped
her wiry arms
around the elder's hips
grinnin up at her

~ **xii** ~
serpentine road
jus down a ways
she spotted dust clouds
crestin the horizon
makin way to her
'58 corsair
papa bought a month ago
brand spankin new
his sweet chariot comin for
to take her home
modest
humble
hard workin he was
second generation sharecropper
family did well ownin land
growin cane and
cantaloupe and cotton
wit modest grove of fig trees
he met forsythia's mama
at market in town one day
laid eyes on her
laid his heart at her feet
and though grandmama
no longer believed in no man
she was taken by this man
so she blessed their union

~ **xiii** ~
sweet chariot came to a stop
and papa stepped out
cap tipped to grandmama and
smilin at his daughter
she held grandmama's hand
steadfastly

first time in her eleven years
she ain't ran into her papa's arms
her heart was regret heavy
leavin grandmama
this strong willed woman
who planted forsythia bushes
celebratin her favorite
grandbaby's arrival
an old southern woman
who rarely smiled
so firm and solemn
wit twinges of sadness in her eyes
a flourishin rose
thorns despite
opened up to forsythia
this particular sunday
and she finally saw
grandmama's softness and warmth

~ **xiv** ~
the elder woman hugged her
as she gave the girl over to papa
proclaimin wit shine in her eyes
promises of greater sundays to come
next time right after church
she gonna have some
cranberry cornbread
fried green tomatoes wit okra
black eye peas
blackened catfish and
sweet potato pie
awaitin her
wit more secrets to share
jus between them
grandmama gave her
love's kiss on her forehead
so on the way
back home wit papa
liniment and amber filled forsythia
wit the warmth of
grandmama's sunshine

~ **:** ~

in tha heat of a day

i sat out unda tha apple tree
and felt tha air streamin past me
coolin tha sweat on my brown skin
grateful for that blessed wind
on my right... a glass of ice water
on my left... a tape recorder
playin smooth sounds of new york jazz
hopin this moment will always last
i shut my eyes and breathe a heavy sigh
it's a quiet day and no cars have driven by
there are chirren runnin and playin in tha street
aint affected by this unyieldin heat
they laugh... they argue... they laugh again
as they play a stickball game tha best they can

i sat on a blanket at tha beach
quietly countin grains of sand one and each
tha wind was at my back... blowin hard
and tha sea so serene without a mar
i sat there wit my radio on loud
listenin to tha music of new york sounds
tha seagulls above me doin supple whirls
and chirren about me... boys and girls
tha boys playfully give tha girls great chase
tha girls squealed... runnin from them in great haste
their smiles and laughta foreva surroundin me
as i realize i don't eva wanna leave

i laid on my bed late at night... naked unda a sheet
wit my fan on tryin to deal wit this heat
tha chirren are in bed now... their day now done
and piercin tha night... tha shot of a gun
i hear tha police sirens answerin that lone call
probably anotha young brotha takin tha fall
for most of tha day anotha time existed
i know it as a fact for in my heart i do miss it
these things i will always hold dear to me
my apple tree... tha chirren... tha serenity of tha sea
but i know anotha day like this will come to pass
and when that day comes i will make it last

~:~

eye blinked... n lost...

about a month ago...
i had this confrontation
on the 4 train...
while headin into work...
it was a most interestin
confrontation...
it tested my mettle
my worth
my... guts, if you will

so i'm bumpin da iPod
(i'm still lovin da 80 gigs...)
positioned near the train doors
nestled comfortably
so that no matter how crowded
or how crushin
i still maintained a modicum
of space, my only frontier...

then at the nevins street stop
and a little unbeknownst to me
my adversary enters
short in stature...
baby phat physique
multiple pony tails
and brown like a chocolate cherry drop
travelin with her mama
all of seven years old
and a lil' precocious...

so I spied her momentarily
out the corner of my peripheral
and she's just chattin away
and her mama, loving her
listened the way mama's do...
patiently with lots of humor...

so i goes back to bumpin my iPod
listenin to talib kweli's liberation album
but then...
I spied eyes...
or actually felt 'em
burnin thru my grill...
and glancin over
I sees the lil chocolate cherry drop

staring at me like chirren do...
like it's their business to...

I look away
thinkin that perhaps she'll find
some other victim to bore holes into but...
alas
she, for some reason, found me interestin...
dissectin me with her unshameful glare
this one got guts, me thinks
but then my ego kicked in...
i'm gonna give it just as much as she's givin it

so i turn and give her my baleful glare
not a frown nor a smile
it's a standoff at the o.k. corral
like the outlaw josey wales vs the magnificent 7
and we're slingin the glares
like two determined souls fightin
for that last spot in heaven...

but then...
but then...
she does the unpardonable...

she
smiles

happily....

and i crumble
like a poorly stacked house of cards
and i giggled as if i was seven again

and for about thirty seconds
she and i held that common bond...
happiness and innocence...

i thank god i lost that battle

i thank god for chocolate cherry drop lil girls who smile like the sun
and remind me that i still smile like the sun as well...

~ **:** ~

ode to k.k.

i saw you
in the last
bit of day -
a surviving patch
of pale blue light
surrounded by
the indigo ink
of the night

~ :: ~

[for Kimmi]

favored child

Favored Child, you are –
with rivers running deep
like hot molten lava stratum
within the Earth's girth.
Shooting straight from the hip
rounds of Mama-Logic and
clips of Grammy-Logic
acquired during years
of study under the loving
tutelage of Matriarchs.
Favored Child, you are –
as strong as titanium...
as fragile as tears...
You ain't ask nobody
to make you their Goddess –
just cuz you were being
YOURSELF.
Just cuz your spirit got there
ten paces before you.
Favored Child,
we all wants to bask
in your glory.
But take care, baby girl.
Don't let no one siphon
your love-energy –
whether it be through their ignorance
or the designs of their own machinations.
Just don't let them!
Take care, girl –
I know you will
cuz you don't play
none of them triflin' games.
Favored Child,
can't they see?
You just a baby girl.
You see, others come to you
with their problems up on their backs
and wearing personal issues
for footwear.
They don't wanna acknowledge your youth.
They're afraid if they
recognize it for what it really is,
you will no longer be that
crutch made out of solid oak
that they likes to lean on
all the damn time.
They're selfish, girl.
But sometimes it's understandable
and it can be flattering...
if it doesn't flatten you first.

Favored Child,
your screaming laugh
is the epiphany of mirth –
laughter from the
soles of your feet,
laughter from the
soul of your spirit.
Causing all kinds of spirits
to join you in the
sweet sounds of joyful release.
Was that the Creator
standing behind you
that I saw?...
Uh-ah, girl!
'Bout to bust out laughin'
along with you – the Favored Child?!
Yeah, I did see Her...
looking proudly at one
of Her better creations.
Favored Child,
you got that healing power
and you don't have to
touch no one physical-like.
You just speak and the
Creator channels through
the breath of your speech
of your songs...
of your love...
And you ain't scared
to take your rightful mantle.
You are aware of the responsibility
cuz you claiming yours!
Claim it, Favored Child!
Claim it, Child of God!
Claim it, Sistah-Girl!
Can't no one but you
claim your rightful due.
Be that wild flower child...
that Soul Super Sistah...
that Diva Delight!
Be all that just for you and only you.
Satisfy those inner desires
that give you reason to
Flourish and Thrive and Shine
like sassy burnished brassy.
And get out those sunglasses, Sistah girl,
cuz your future's really bright.
Cuz it boils down to it
being all about you, girl.
It's all about the Favored Child

~ :: ~

[for Shelley]

19

open appreciation

we can act like it ain't true
but deep down
we want some form of acknowledgement
that we are loved or even thought of
from time to time.
it may have stemmed since
the moment we were conceived
because of the immediate connection
with our birth-givers
or maybe we are beings
that have a sort of
inherent pack mentality...
we all have this need to
bond & build & thrive.
so when that one person
from outta the blue
thinks of you...
gives you a gift that satisfies
you intellectual interests,
makes your favorite meal,
takes you out to your favorite spot,
or devotes a caring ear to you
in your most desperate hour of need...
it is a blessing beyond all blessings
& you can not help but
express your exuberance
because it bubbles to the top
past all defenses & boundaries,

exposing you to the fact
that an unspoken need or desire
has been satisfied.
so i just wanted to let you know
that it brings me pleasure
when you are pleased.
it satisfies the benevolence
that my spirit craves.
it is a compelling sensation
beyond ordinary explanations.
it is one of the many aspects
of a divine universal unfettered love
that i can fully indulge.
it reinforces the knowing
that there is more good in the world
than there is of bad.
the scales are righteously tipped.
so i thank you
for this glorious moment of
opening, sharing, caring & laughter.
i thank you for the exchange
of mental, spiritual &
emotional nourishment.
i thank you for feeling safe enuf with me
and allowing me
to facilitate and contribute
to your joy and growth
as you have so willingly done for me.

~:~

verse 2

~:~

iowaikus

haiku is a form of poetry that originated from the japanese culture. it is a great exercise in communicating effectively with the least amount of words. the pattern of a haiku is 5/7/5, the amount of syllables per line, with a 3 line total. a traditional form of haiku usually links a human condition with nature.

but to be completely honest, my haikus are not that disciplined... which is why i call them "iowaikus" (pronounced eye~oh~why~koos). i still follow the 17 syllable form and still break it down to the total 3 lines, but i'm conveying my concepts and thoughts like a needle of verbal dope straight to the brain...

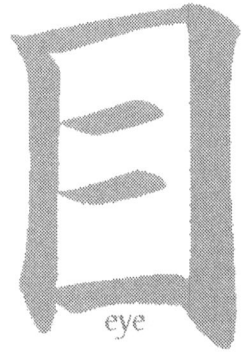

目
eye

12:16:04

he loosed my stuck up
so my rapture is only
for his smiling eyes

~:~

飲む
drink

06:03:05

drinking liquid gold.
from his mouth - love's libation
saturates my soul.

~ :: ~

口

mouth

06:14:05

i just wanna kiss
the sky with these lips that have
kissed you lovingly.

~:~

港

tongue

06:17:05

spring day's morning touch.
i suck coffee off his tongue.
i am awakened.

-::-

怪我

hurt

07:10:06

i love men so much,
that it is so hard to hate
them when they fuck up.

~:: ~

深い
deep

08:04:06

your abandonment
issues run deeper than you
admit...excavate

~:!:~

木

tree

05:28:07

stripping your Self bare
shows vulnerability
and reveals True You.

~ :: ~

太陽

sun

08:28:06

your spirited eyes
is sunrise glimmering off
the ocean's surface

~ :: ~

想像力

imagination

08:29:06

crushin aint easy...
verbal stimuli entice
final fantasy.

~:~

話す

speak

09:04:06

don't know if he means
half the things he says but his
talkin sure sounds fine

~:!:~

尻

booty

09:28:06

perspective: he says
my ass is too big... but i
say his dick's too short.

~ :: ~

馬鹿
fool

10:03:06

denial, you've dwelled.
your house of cards have crumbled.
bullshit in ruins.

~:~

誠実
honesty

10:03:06

insecurity:
it is best assessed with the
eyes of honesty.

~ •• ~

恐い
fearful

10:03:06

insecurity:
know that fear is a damn lie.
tap into your strength.

~:~

人材

capable

10:26:06

it wasn't until
i became an ASSET that
i was at last seen.

~ :: ~

洗脳
brainwashing

10:31:06

we are conditioned
as children to mind thought but
not to think mindly.

~:: ~

戦
争
war

11:09:06

why do we argue
with people that don't matter?
hopeless non-cypher.

~ :: ~

毒

poison

11:16:06

chaining the spirit:
rules that do not allow for
flexibility.

~ :: ~

泣く

cry

04:30:07

beware of women
with no female friends at all...
self-misogynous.

~ :: ~

嘘

lie

05:12:07

a half truth always
equals a whole fuckin lie...
so, who you foolin?

~ :: ~

verse 3

~:: ~

the back hand side

i once sat in a women's circle about ten years ago. there was about twenty of us and the moderator of that circle asked a very tough question to us all... the question was: "how many of you sistas have ever been sexually abused by a family member?"

but what was tougher was to witness that out of nearly twenty of us, only three sistas and i didn't raise our hands and that cold stoned blew my mind. 80% of those women were abused... by a family, no less! that was the first time that reality fucked with my head and my heart hasn't stopped crying for those sistas and others beyond that ever since.

although i was blessed to have the family that i was born into, there are those sistas that are not as fortunate and never get the chance to speak and voice their pain and anger. this verse is for those unheard voices... hotep.

d.o.v.d. juxtaposed

depression is depressing
oppression is oppressing
victimization is victimizing
degradation is degrading

depression is degrading
oppression is depressing
victimization is oppressing
degradation is victimizing

depression is victimizing
oppression is degrading
victimization is depressing
degradation is oppressing

depression is oppressing
oppression is victimizing
victimization is degrading
degradation is depressing

depression is depressing
oppression is oppressing
victimization is victimizing
degradation is degrading

~:~

the baby, she cries

the baby, she cries
for all the lies
chucked her way - -
spear tipped bones
piercing tender skin.
she balls into a
fetal position - -
position fatal - -
embalmed in pain.
trust was the
double edge sword
that cleaved her soul
into halves
and now she
haves...not.
her love is
poisoned water
to the thirsty beast
that is she - -
drainage from
her sieved spirit,
infected with
verbose arsenic /
accentuated with
the touch of
slow death - -
dying, dying & dying...
crying, crying & crying...

the baby, she cries
muted tears
which mutates
into post drama trauma
that none but
she & God
understands - -
and barely
do she comprehends
and even less
do she face
the erratic dancing
of baneful imps
on the periphery
of her awareness.
vile creatures
whose strength
increases with every
bad word
and with every
bad touch
administered by
lost souls
deceptively disguised
as mama & papa
who purchased
whole chunks of
real estate
in the misguided
vicious circle of hate
funneled thru ignorance.

the baby, she cries
as her man slaps her
once more...
slaps her once more...
slaps her once more...
infusing love with pain
and deeper yet, she's
confusing love with pain
and it is more
than she can sustain,
but her reality knows
no other way
for life to be real.
she can only
identify pain
with love
because those
that she loved
gave her pain - -
and it made sense
in conjunction with her
jaded existence.
no one dared
to interfere
in her early days.
now everybody
looks in countless
other directions in her
later days.
face her they could not cuz
family don't wanna see
the ugly done to her - -
with their set chins,
their stiff upper lips,
and some friends choose to be
stone cold blind at best.

the baby, she cries
for she dies
a thousand deaths
plus one
and now her days
are done.
the baby, she cries
for now she lies
six feet deep
and ironically
her friends and family
now weeps.
the baby, she cries
for there was no answer
to "why?"
and for her soul
there is no rest
for sorrow has made
a nest
of her broken heart

~ :: ~

who is to blame?

it was just something to do...
getting married and saying 'i do'...
it was just something to do.

they didn't love each other,
they didn't respect each other,
they didn't even really enjoy having sex with each other.

he, a trifling nigger,
she, a disillusioned niggress,
who both had little or no self esteem
as they practiced in the fine arts of nigrification.

he did not love himself,
she did not love herself
and they both believed that with little or none of the proper equipment,
they could make the marriage workable.

what was their basis?

surely not his parents
cuz they never did get married,
though his mama had many babies by the same man
and surely not her parents
cuz her papa left her mama when she was young
and her mama's 2nd husband became a casualty of the drug war by way of an
unclean syringe in a darkened alley.

neither one had been exposed to stability,
neither one had a proper foundation to stand on.

sometimes...
sometimes...
sometimes...
she would contemplate a divorce from his evil ass
but over the years, she had become complacent in her marriage with him.

and he?
regardless, marriage had never stopped him from getting pussy –
either hers or some other's.
it made no matter.
he had, however, vague memories of caring for her once,
but that was what they were - vague memories.

she couldn't deny all these bad things about him
for she knew of his extra - marital activities.
she even acquired a couple of male friends outside her marriage as well,
to lessen the pain of rejection...frustration...and no love.

so why bothered being with him?
deep down,
when no one was listening closely,
she would ask herself that question,
and quickly turn away before she could face the answer.

he... well,
he never did bothered asking that question.
he never bothered asking any questions
in life
about life
or for life.
he pretty much did what he damn well pleased -
as long as the instant gratification was worth it
cuz there was nothing more thrilling than living for the moment.

another hobby of his that he had acquired
was keeping her under his thumb.

each and every time she needed his help,
he would tell her 'no!',
then watched as she pleaded for his help piteously.
and when he finally conceded, he would always say:
'damn it! you better not ask me to do this shit for you again!'
but it would go on:
the vicious cycle that it was
she wouldn't stop asking for his help.
he wouldn't stop making her beg.
she wouldn't stop begging.
he wouldn't stop feeding off the feeling of power.

and what was truly scary was that
things won't change a damn bit,
that these two were in it for the long haul.
she'll continue to complain to her friends...
they'll comfort her and tell her 'He's a fucking dog'
then encourage her in the same breath to be as bad as he
and find other men to be with.
he'll continue to disregard her and do what he pleased,
regardless of how she may feel.
they were both victims
they were both perpetrators
they were both complacent.
neither one would seriously be done with it.
tell me, who is to blame?

~:~

if only you chose to see

i saw you
through your battered,
black and blue,
swollen eye...
the left...
girl, i saw you
as you would see yourself
through that bruised orb
as you primped in front of the mirror
in your bathroom,
ignoring its soreness
and what it really
represented.
denying the action
that was done
unto you to cow you,
allowing love to be
redefined into a more
brutal, sadistic, heinous definition.
they say love is blind.
i guess it is
when love is the fist
that shuts down all
your systems.
but check it, girl -
you have one
good eye remaining
...the right...
there still is
a good chance
that you will still
be able to see
before the fist of love
comes again like the blight
and smite your existence.
there is still...
a good chance...
can't you see?
why don't you see?
i take another peek
through that battered orb
and I saw you standing still,
holding yourself tightly
with fear in your eyes.
i saw a dim light
of understanding
on your face.

you realized
what you must do,
but you're frozen
like a deer caught
in the headlights.
Run! Run!
Go on girl!
Run!
Save yourself!
What the hell are you
standing there for!!!!!
Shit!!!!! Girl, run!!!!
but something told me
to look in your good eye,
the one yet untouched.
so I did.
and as I looked
i saw how you beheld
this destroyer in the guise
of a man -
as if he was
some kind of
perverted divine being
that can give your existence
some kind of meaning.
perhaps because
you were never given
the tools necessary
to give yourself some
meaning.
or maybe
you were taught
that in order
to give yourself
some meaning,
you have to allow
drama into the peace
of your realm.
i did, for you
the one thing that
you probably haven't done
for yourself.
i cried.
i cried red, hot angry tears.
i cried deep sorrowful tears.
i cried these tears for you,
Sistah-Girl...

but what can be done
for someone who doesn't
wish to see?
what can be done
for someone who
wishes to one turn
one bad blind eye,
for fear that the good one
will be taken away as well?
i saw all of this
though your eyes.
i saw two sides
of the same fucking story.
i saw ALL this craziness.
but you didn't want to see.
you deliberately kept
your bruised eye blinded
due to the jaded experiences
and you deliberately kept
your good eye blinded
due to the
kaleidoscopic dreams
all administered by
this destroyer
in the guise of a man.
YOU!
it all boiled down to *YOU!*
so i realized that
it wouldn't mattered
how much i wanted
to slaughter that
filthy bastard
in the name of
sisterhood
or
how much i wanted
be there for you
to rub salve
on your black, blue
and angry red bruises
or
how much i wanted
to cry, for you, rivers
of lava hot tears
to help wash away
your fears.
what truly mattered

in your reality
is that you would have to be
the one to face your
demons -
whether they are
past demons from a
poor childhood
of broken dreams
and empty promises
or
present demons
that walk and talk
like a man but
damn sure don't
act like a real man.
it's all on you,
Sistah-Girl...
cuz truly,
shit ain't gonna
get done unless
you want it to get done.
we all know this.
even that hell-spawn
that you call "my man" knows this.
and he knows that
as long as you choose
to be in this
poor excuse for drama
called LIFE,
you're giving him
carte blanche to use
your beautiful body
as a punching bag.
girl, if you really
and truly loved yourself,
you'd run
with only the change
in your pocket and
determination in your heart
never to look back
ever again...

~••~

fantasy nightmare sin

the vision to have him always seems to be so clear at first - precise and to the point...from point A to point B. but it's not until hindsight when it is realized how narrow the scope really is. love at first sight is blind. attraction takes flight with seemingly flawless breath. it is uninhibited, mystical and exciting to just imagine lips pressed against your own. the exchanging of moisture and air flows in passages long deprived of such reverie. the feel and want and naked yearning of his sex mingled with your own. it is sheer torture just to be in his presence and not throw yourself on his tracks head on in front of his express train of movements, flows and momentums. but the fantasy is oh so exhilarating to play over and over in your mind. the connection so smooth that you can not or will not distinguish the end from the beginning nor the beginning from the end.

and so it is sin.

the sin of being so close, yet so far. the real, legitimate fear of rejection. that you've been a little obsessive to be in his presence. but what's burning on the other end of your candle is that nagging fear of being alone, floating in limbo in a non state of being. and this has got you terrified and this is why you fight so hard to avoid the loss of him, while failing to realize that you've already lost him because you've never really found yourself.

~ :: ~

his thorny kiss stings me so my bloodstained lips become a testament of sacrificial offerings in his name.

the touch of him burns icy hot upon my tender skin and marks me his – love/hate tattoos scarring me for life.

as he gazes into my eyes, the windows of my universe, he reaches in and snuffs out all my stars and leaves me in still darkness.

his penetration is sans intimacy, instead it is a constant rhythm of assault; a machine gun that gives a barrage of acidic sperm and sears the lining of my womb.

words spoken and unspoken stitches my primary eye closed with raggedy sutures leaving dreams and hops beaming between the cracks – a breath beyond the touch of my fingertips, a gasp beyond my breath.

as well my words are his unspoken thoughts, whispered clandestinely into my ear, while others looked elsewhere.

I speak not my words, but falsely.

the will to live is not strong enough, nor the will to die, so I hang in limbo.

suspended like a marionette, making movement only when he firmly tugs at my strings.

my steps are faltered, my dance is stinted.

neither natural nor free flowing.

so I cease to be...

...and breathe only when he breathes...

externalization

insecurities givin birth to accusations
blinded by fear and unresolved issues
evolvin into the green eyed monster of funkenstein
force feedin his ugliness into her free spirit
he wanted to make her feel as dirty as he felt
cuz he didn't want to take the responsibility...
cuz he didn't want to take the action...
to get up off his fuckin ass
and fix his shit until it was as right as rain
he punished his woman cuz he couldn't forgive himself
so he strove to make her unforgivable
misery is always lookin for company to keep... on lock down
he felt less than a man (and deep down a lesser man always feel
that he is never enough to satisfy his woman)
so he accuses her of cheatin to attempt to make her out to be the discordant one
he insists her eyes & hips & lips
always wandered to the next man
when he wasn't around her
(but what was he doin behind her back?)
no matter that she has faithfully stood by his side through his turbulent times
strivin to keep his spirits up
while he drained her light like an emotional vortex
he wanted her to be as miserable as he
so he can justify treatin her like shit
cuz she was tangible and that made her easy to grasp
unlike his issues
and often they have grappled –
she sportin bruises tattooed upon arms and back
where he grabbed and slammed her into the entertainment cabinet
while he wore deeply furrowed scratches on face, neck and arms
where she fought back like an alley cat
he didn't want to fix his shit so she fixed it for him
911 and a size 8 boot to the ass
locks changed and attitude switched
she was fed up with bein worn and torn down
isolated from friends and family
in order to satisfy his insatiable and bruised self-esteem
where he didn't want to take responsibility for himself, she took it for herself
where he didn't want to take action for himself, she took it for herself
regainin and reclaimin her power
cuz she'd be damned
if she was to go down that same road that he chose to
and end up trapped in a livin hell

~ :: ~

subterfuge

confusin infatuation
wit reality...
fittin square pegs
inta round holes...
becomin an emotional chameleon...
neglectin self needs...
ova lookin tha signals
uv smoke dats
screenin agendas hidden...
convinced uv tha
psycho-non-logical
rhetoric
snakin
frum his lips
eager to lie ta myself
so i can lie wit him
in a bed uv
denial and deceit...
my reception ta deception
was wit
no fight or flight
jus fancies
uv my
fleetin imagination...
afraid regurgitation
uv tha bullshit
i willingly consumed
will scorch
my parched spirit
on its way back up
an taste 10x as bad
when i choke it back down...
so my
desperation fa justification
like noose ta neck
got me hangin
and swangin
on his every word
like it mattered more
than my own

life
happiness
strength...
jus cuz
i fear
bein alone
common sense is long gone
somewhere buried deep
in dark cavernous recesses...
suppressed truth abscesses
blisterin inta mental illnesses...
lookin
soundin
feelin
unhealthy...
stumblin
falterin
thru life...
i have become
strife
personified...
self-perpetrated assault
ta my essence...
forgiveness i seek
when eyes meet
upon gazin at
my exhausted reflection...
tha queen starin
right back
deserves her redemption...
tha guilt will
continue to flourish
tha more i nourish
it wit dread + time
so i gotta
start somewhere
to end this sickness...
why not here and
why not now...?

~•••~

suiciDaL TeNDeNcies

eVery Time i see ya
i geTs a NerVous Tick
ya kNow, rigHT BeLow m'LeFT eye
aND m'waLk geTs kiNDa gimPisH -
you Lousy cHeese smeLLiN' raT BasTarD!
i waNNa cHoke ya wiT' your owN eNTraiLs!
i sTiLL HaVe THose ViViD memories
oF wHeN ya PuT me THrougH THose cHaNges
cuz oF THaT craZy BiTcH
you was seeiN' BeHiND m'Back.
eVeN HaD THe NerVe To
BriNg Her To m'House
TaLkiN' aBouT you were
goNNa LeT Her kick my ass!
ya BesT BeLieVe i broke BoTH yo asses THaT Day!
some "maN" you TurNeD ouT To Be!
PuT me THrougH mo' cHaNges
THaN a Drag queeN DoiN' a sHow.
TeLLiN' me i aiN'T sHiT!
PusHiN' me To THe BriNk oF
suiciDaL TeNDeNcies!
maDe me HaTe myseLF.
BuT guess wHaT, you wasTe oF sPerm?
i reaLiZeD THaT you DamN sure DiDN'T LoVe me!
sHiT! you BareLy LoVeD yo'seLF!
aN' uNForTuNaTeLy i aiN'T LearNeD To LoVe myseLF
eNougH!
BuT i LoVe myseLF Now!
aN' kNowiN' THaT - THe Tick LeaVes aN' my waLk is
NormaL.

Fuck you.

~ :: ~

ode to frank

*"to survive myself,
i forge you,
like a weapon,
like an arrow in my bow,
a stone in my sling."*
~pablo neruda

unfortunately, i let you in –
trusted you and gave you
my secret code words to
my inner sanctum,
which you infiltrated with ease
to lay the explosive charges.
you blew a hole in my being
and left your residue on the
shrapnel of my inner pain.
i almost hated myself
as much as i hated you
when you imploded my tender spirit
and left me stone cold wounded.
you made me see that side
of me that i was not ready to
face – that weak side.
so now to survive myself,
i scrape your residue from
my inner pain's shrapnel,
much like a scientist collecting
radioactive samples –
i collect it all, to separate
my pain from your hate.
and like a blacksmith,
i will forge your hate
into a weapon of my choosing –
and send it back to its maker
to drive it straight through
your darkened heart.

~:.~

57

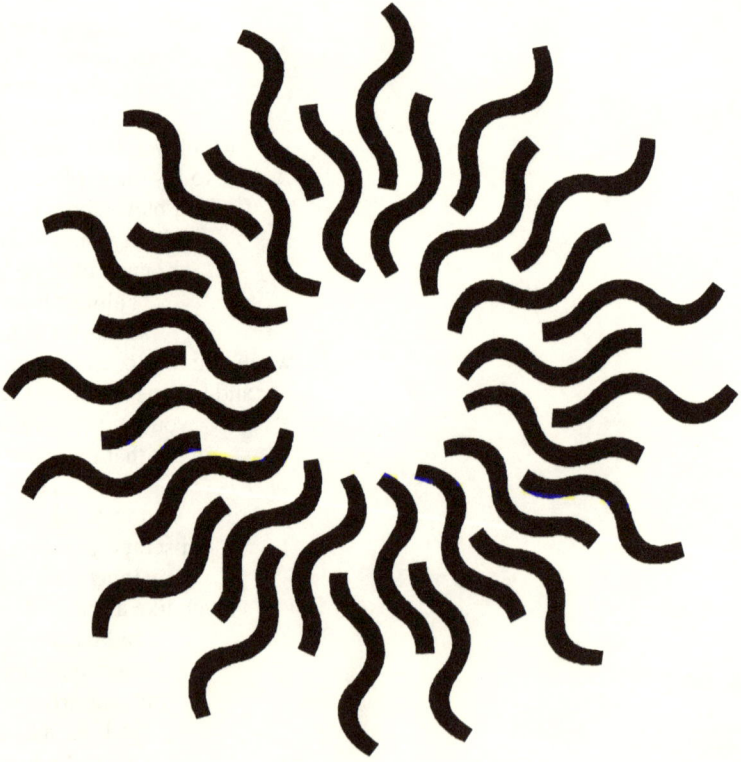

verse 4

~ :: ~

blue tenements

street life is an existence led by a gritty code that i, at moments, have difficulty in decyphering. there are rules and laws that makes no sense to me and causes me sorrow just to witness at first hand.

these words in this verse can only convey the scenes of street life that i've laid eyes to... poetic documentation from a stream of consciousness that fights just as hard as the denizens of the streets to understand the psychosis of it all.

the players of the street life in the end, as in the beginning, are only humans. they fight to survive within the confines of chaos. what is considered a win or a loss is entirely subjective... but it never lessens the fight...

a bullet with your name on it

there's a bullet with your name on it.
and who could you blame on it?
can't you see the old game of it?
run, nigger, run! Hide, nigger, hide!
trigger pulled! cap popped! Now baby is gonna die!
six inches of hard, cold, steel dick by your side.
.357 bores a hole in flesh ten miles wide.
another brother crumbles to the floor,
a child cut in two, his soul at Death's door.
and who is the true enemy?
A pig? A crumbsnatcher? A bitch? Another nigger?
who was the evil that pulled that trigger?
it don't matter when the lights are out... they all fit that shape.
using Death's cold instrument that was created by hate.
and as that bullet with your name on it begins to fly,
you'll probably find no answer as you begin to die.

~ :: ~

dedicated to the brother shot at the
Vibe Club February 10, 1995 between 2:00 & 3:00 a.m.

vial luv

ah crak vial
stuk 'n ah sidewalk crak
discard'd by crak'd fingatips
manip'lat'd by ah crak'd mind
emmersed 'n crack'd perceptions
her inna sanctum crak'd
she enta'd ah crak'd compound
paid toll for anotha crak'd cloud high
as cumulus thunda roll'd 'n crak'd 'n term-oil
with'n her junkie crakpot mentality
da ride too strong - her heart crak'd
she slipped limply thru da crak cumulus
fallin' bak ta reality - body crak'd upon 'mpact
frail, brittle, splinta'd by assidic crak
her remains stuk 'n a sidewalk crak -
nex' to her demonic luv'r - a crak vial

~ ⁖ ~

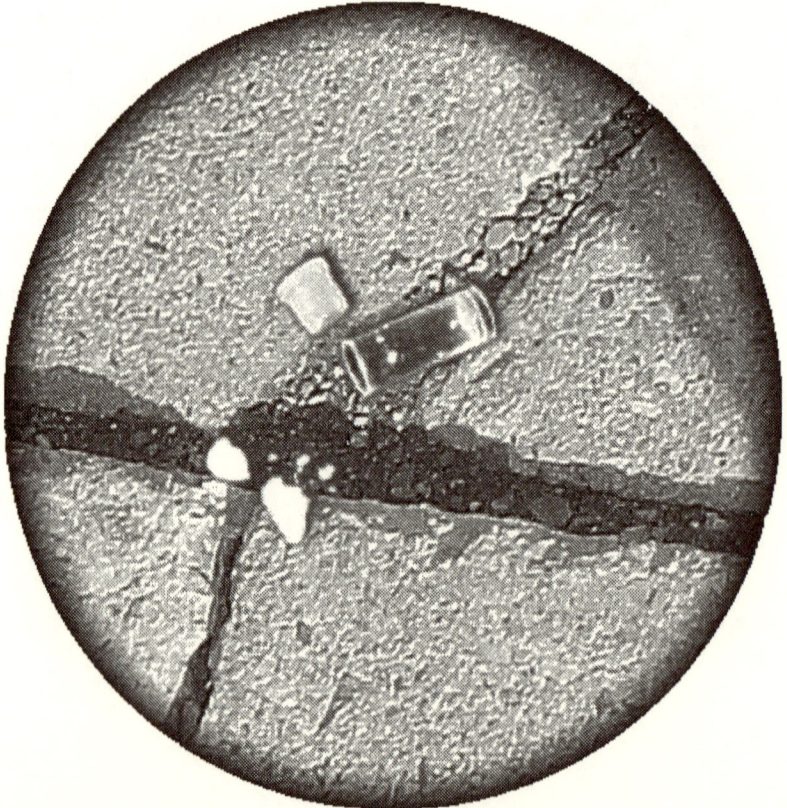

scarlett harlot / sugar babie

scarlett harlot on forty-deuce
once was called sugar babie
with pink bubblicious dreams.
now the stardom ain't what it seems.

eyes shadowed to conceal agony.
blushed covered repetitively
bruised cheeks.
lips once pettily pouty,
now beat down puffy,
lined with saccharin sweet
pimp mama lies
as she lies sugar babie down
and rapes her dreams,
and rapes her ideals,
and rapes her will to fight;
injecting heroin cut
with fear and worthlessness
into a terrified girl's veins.
she devolved into her slave -
pimp mama's sugar babie slave.
she peeled away nearly all
this child's being -
skinned her like a seedless grape,
a little at a time was how
pimp mama raped.

scarlett pounds the pavement
like her heart pounds her chest.
indifference was her breath
...on the outside.
inside sugar babie cries
for the sweet release of being
a young, vibrant girl once again.
she holds on tightly to what was
because deep deep deep inside

she believed that life
would always come full circle.
she believed that her
chance as a young
carefree girl
would come again.

sugar babie was not far
from the truth -
life always did come full circle.
but for various reasons,
she would miss her chances:
a hit of the horse to
diminish the shakes,
pimp mama doing
demolition work
on any suspected
budding hopes of escape,
the need to have food and clothes
for the child that she fooled
herself into thinking
that he didn't know
what his mama does...
she constantly missed her chances
to be part of the circle of life
once again.

scarlett harlot on forty-deuce
once was called sugar babie
with pink bubblicious dreams.
now the stardom ain't what it seems.

they laid on their sides
with her back to his front,
his arms encircled her waist,
scarlett's eyes staring at the night stand
where a ripped and crumpled
condom wrapper resided next to
the hundred dollar bill,
his watch and his bifocal glasses.
he whispered to her:
"you're too beautiful to be in this
business."
she laid there listless and
in her mind, she thought:
"i use to be beautiful. sugar babie sweet

...but now I am ugly and trapped."
he whispered again:
"you're too beautiful to be in this
business."
she thought:
"I use to be beautiful. sugar babie sweet
...but now I am ugly and trapped."
"you're too beautiful to be in this business."
"i use to be beautiful. sugar babie sweet..."
"you're too beautiful to be in this."
"i use to be beautiful..."
"you're too beautiful."
"...*...*...*..." she falters.
"you're too beautiful...say it!"
she turns and gives him
a measured look.
"say it!"
"i...am...beautiful..." she whispers.
"believe it." he says quietly.
he rises, dresses and leaves.
he leaves sugar babie with
budding hopes and dreams...
once again...

sugar babie's not crying anymore.
she's smilin'
and scarlett feels the elation
despite the residue of the
smack highs from the night before.
she hums as she packs
a couple of bags of clothes
for her son and herself.
you see, pimp mama never knew
about the money she managed
to squirrel away.
somehow sugar babie kept
scarlett from giving up
that bit of information.
no matter how much heroin
scarlett craved for
from pimp mama,
sugar babie fought to keep
scarlett's trap shut.
"no more!" she pleads desperately.
"everything's gonna be
good, i promise you.

it ain't gonna be easy,
but we will be alright."
it was alright but
it wasn't always easy being alright.
she had to swallow her pride
when she found herself
back at her papa's doorstep.
when she left chasing dreams
with a butterfly net,
she left as a rosy cheeked young girl.
now she came back a haggard ol' bitch,
nearly dead on her feet,
with a ten year old son at her side.
but Papa loved her and he forgave her
and he loved her some more.
he missed her too much
to even waste precious time with anger.
he held her tightly when she
had dry heaves from the
lack of smack.
he held her hand
when she was tested for
all kinds of diseases.
he was there for scarlett
until she was there 100%
for herself and her boy.
and one day, papa looked
into scarlett's eyes and
saw sugar babie looking
back at him and whispered:
"my...baby's...back!"
all sugar babie can do
was smile.
and she never stopped smilin' since.

scarlett harlot's gone away now cuz
sugar babie's smilin' deep
with pink bubblicious dreams.
and now her spirit's flying free!

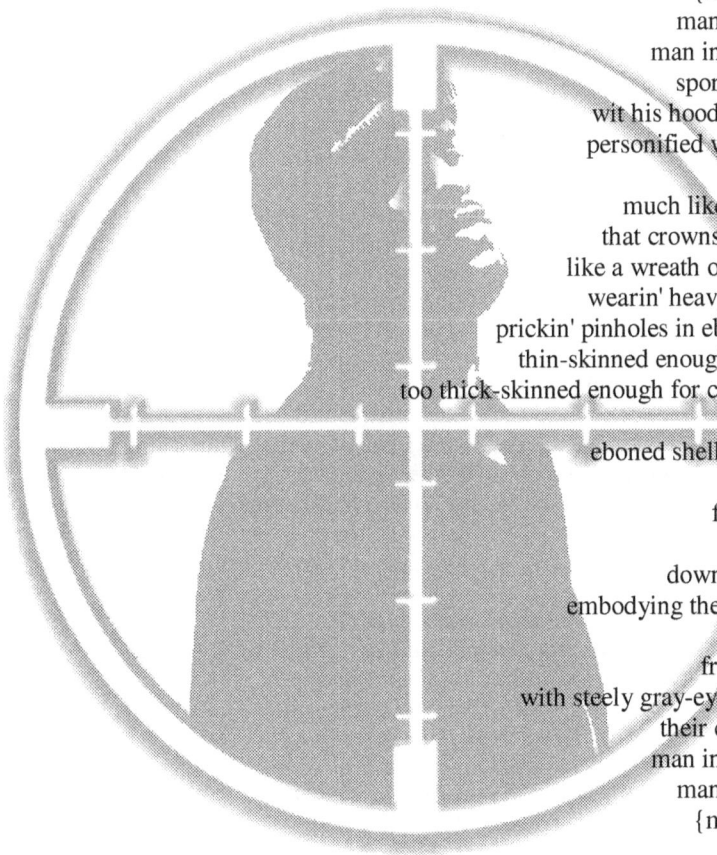

manhood
{man [hood] lum]
manhood / hoodlum
man in hood lumberin'
sportin' hoodee gear
wit his hood winked ideals -
personified wool pulled over
half-slitted orbs
much like the knitted cap
that crowns his dome-piece
like a wreath of societal thorns
wearin' heavy upon his brow
prickin' pinholes in eboned epidermis
thin-skinned enough for infiltration
too thick-skinned enough for comprehension...
perhaps
eboned shell seen as a target
duck, he does,
from side to side
as he be-bops
down asphalt dreams
embodying the darkest colours
as camouflage
from blue hunters
with steely gray-eyed night sights -
their crosshairs set on
man in hood lumberin'
manhood / hoodlum
{man [hood] lum]
manhood.

~ :: ~

when the clock struck thirteen...

you, dear "brother", want me to understand you plight? you need me to understand how hard it is for a Black Man in this society? this white society?

but how can i understand your plight when you rolled up on my sister and roused her for her knapsack?

in fact...i can't even think to call you a "brother" because BROTHER is a righteous title and you ain't right. you're just an infiltrator in brown skin.

NO! NO! NO! my love just ain't infinite enough for perpetrators like you. i can't believe you would expect that from me. where was your love for my sister who you victimized?

my love is precious and tender and protective. protective of my sister that ya ass rolled up on.

sometimes i don't wanna see this. but your demonic actions have forced me to prop toothpicks up to keep my eyelids steady open so that I don't sleep, won't sleep on punk muthafucks like you. cuz i'm lookin to discern you from the true BROTHERS.

i wanna offer you up as that strange fruit that Lady Day sangs about hangin from the poplar trees. let your corpse dry out in the sun. then serve you up as dog bait for the five-oh.

here's a bit of irony: the merciless asking for mercy - - "ain't we all Black folk? ain't we all sis and bro...?" you will probably cry as a noose that was woven by the hands of your own actions slip like silken lingerie around that scraggly neck of yours and the faces of all your victims stand before you.

pain driven reality.

you'll probably cry those big crocodile tears but you will cry them alone. because before i shed nary a tear for a "brother" gone wrong - - misguided, misdirected, victim/predator, some mother's/father's bad ass/grown ass demon child - - i will shed them for my sister that you rolled up on and knocked to the ground, just for a fuckin knapsack. you and that sorry sack of shit that you call your compadre.

> *the two-man hit team*
> *swells from the darkness of fort greene*
> *dealin with the trouble unseen*
> *and with actions quite unclean*
> *as they accosted my sister-queen*
> *her belongings they have gleamed*
> *for they have worked a scheme*
> *to harvest the easy cream*
> *when the clock struck thirteen...*
> *when the clock struck thirteen...*
> *when the clock struck...*

and so now i am stuck...

because now as i watch the ten o'clock news and I see that african or latino brother being led by the cops to the squad car with their family and friends moaning, "not my baby! he's innocent!", i wonder what is the REAL story. is he innocent or is he cryin wolf only to get out and become that wolf again to prowl and hunt once more on the darkened streets...

~ :: ~

66

blessed

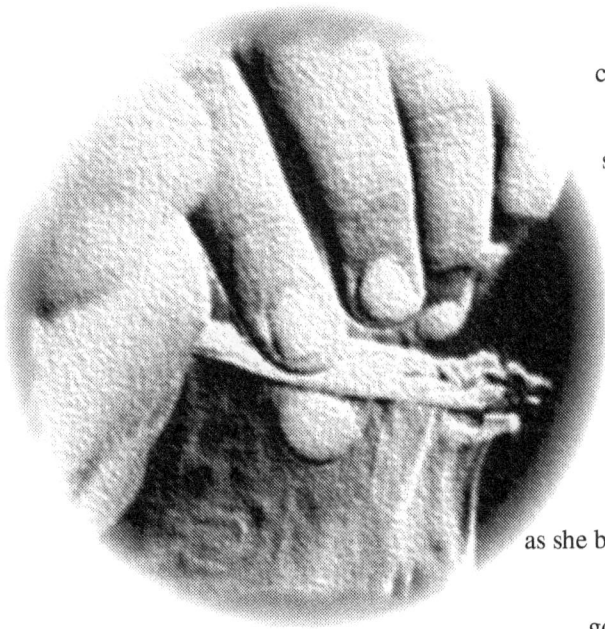

she was blessed
from Buddha-Sess...
mariJane moltov cocktails
trace trails
like snails...
slow burnin bombshell
within her bein
an she's seein
tha profound
as she looks around
an hears tha sounds of
voices inside my head...
so it said...
tha Sacred Buddha-Sess
made a mess
causin her brains to abscess
wit incoherent thoughts...
her rationale fought...
she became overwrought...
but Buddha-Sess was a
Dread-juggernaut...
wit surgical steel-skill
it didn't kill...
jus broke tha will
wit precise precision
annihilatin her decision
to say not...
mental mind meldins
got her meltin
like tha ice on tha hot...
but she cannot stop
as she bonds wit tha cosmic slop...
Buddha-Sess rocked her
from crown to crotch...
got her playin hop-scotch - -
hoppin through smoked hoops
doin loopy-loops
while bein stewed
in this hazy-lazy primordial soup...
she took another puff
to call its bluff
but Buddha-Sess was tuff...
thru ages of existence
its persistence
was sharper than ginzu
dullin tha senses...

~ :: ~

oblivion

slow-eyed death, he is.
finer than any man
that i have witnessed.
but his eyes are inert –
dim and meaningless.
his brain is stained
and missing the point.
claiming he *could* stop
at any time...
the anthem of the addict.
the man he was
has long since gone.
and in his place,
a zombie resurrected
from the dark angel's
cracked dust.
liquefied and infused
into his veins
to mingle and corrupt
his life-force.
leaving scarred tracks –
signs of what domain
he now inhabits.
he has no control
and he is fooling himself
into believing he do.

the poison, instead,
controls him,
which has him out of bounds
and lying to himself.
words spoken from
numbed lips paints dull
visions of defecation and waste.
thoughts congealing to no matter
cuz it don't matter
from this shit-talker.
realizing that they have
finally turned a blind eye
to his false promises & ramblings
of making better of himself,
he professes *fuck them*-s
angrily in their wake
but now even as he
releases his mouth
to spout these infected words
they carry no weight as they
float off into nothingness,
leaving him in angst,
never to achieve the peace
that his dying spirit
is crying for

~ :: ~

broken peeples

i don't deal wit' no broken down
peeples
to' down from lack of passion
fire done died long ago
an' dey eyes reflect
da empty shells dat dey is
broken
shatter'd like glass
standin' on da corner
or sittin' on dey ass
talkin' dat shit
cuz dat's all dey wanna do
mo' alcohol than blood
done flowed thru dey veins
mo' chronic than air
done filled dey lungs
eyes half slit
throat raw
gait slant'd
fingernails crack'd an' stain'd
barely functionin' zombies
mo' than willin' to suck you in
mo' than willin' to suck you dry
broken peeples
emanciat'd goddesses
an' prideless warriors
distort'd an' twist'd
wit' dim, dim mem'ries
of what use ta be
dey purpose is now
ta remind me where i can't go
an' it's sad cuz
dey still my peeples...
jus' broken...
beyond repair

~:~

the art of annihilation

bullets sprayed graffiti
d.n.a. tagged tha sidewalk
final signature rite
stop-motioned runnin
was not enuf 2 escape
becoming fallen macabre artwork
2 inches from tha street's gutta
a broken marionette
discarded
as if santa muerte
(outta sheer folly)
decided 2 sever tha ties
that bound him 2 life
blood seeped slowly
methodical movement of mass exodus
a deep ruby reservoir gatherin
where chest rest on warm pavement
this death imprint
was all it came 2
a misguided young warrior
runnin with otha lost boyz
immersed in static noize
who is now displayed
as a casualty of statistical war
4 public viewin only
birthed on tha wrong side of tha battle
endured on tha wrong side of life
hung on tha wrong side of the street corna

      ...no longa...

this raw aggression
this renderin that intimidate generations
and imitates spiritual obliteration
where brutha gun down brutha
in tha glory of massive genocidal mortification
this vile expression is what
art aficionados have named
"collateral damage maximum"
subtitle "no survivors necessary..."

~:~

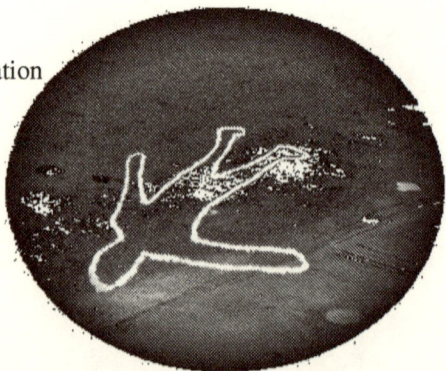

the rumble at franklin ave station...

WARRIORS! COME OUT TO PLAY-YAY....
WARRIORS! COME OUT TO PLAY-YAY....
WARRIORS! COME OUT TO PLAY-YAY....

luther's screeched wurds tauntin
echoin in the back of my cranium
and i can hear those bottles clackin
like castanets made in the ghetto
as i got out of the second train car
at my stop - franklin ave...
the trigger for the mental richochet
a commotion... a rumble... or maybe
someone just gettin their ass whupped
don't know what started it
but at one critical point
it almost ended on the railroad tracks
fallin and rollin precariously
to the edge of the platform
(yo, 'member that scene
when the fox met his end
on the 72nd station tracks?)
blows bein dealt
kicks bein launched
bags obscenely strewn about
conductor can't shut them doors
cuz bro's body was half in/half out
and mufuckas watchin
like it's ali vs frasier...
(yo, sun, pass dat popcorn
and hand me my brew...)
"ohhhhh!" the spectators groaned massively
collectively leanin back as if
they all took that last kick
that the fallen brotha had took
right in their own crotches
it was the most insane shit
i had ever seen in some time
like i said before...
i don't know what started it
and the shit was truly brutal
but what really made it insane...?
folks just stood around
with no care for their safety
let alone for the cat whose
ass was bein tromp on...
no one was tryin to be help...
no one was tryin to get help...
and keep in mind
you just don't know
what mufuckas are packin...

why stand around takin
on the chances of catchin
bullets???
or shiv to the gut???
or brass knucks to the grill???
or a swung bat to the dome???
('member dem furies? swing and a missssss....
but maybe not this time...)
the curiosity is just as morbid
as the public beatdown
and all this i took in while
workin to make tracks
up them stairs
the only one to leave
that gladiator arena
in disgust with a twinge
of fear and sadness...
as i quickly and adeptly
maneuvered myself past
that one-celled, single minded
massive amoeba
in fear that someone will
lose their life...
sadness at how deep
this wound runs
within our broken peeples...
i told the chick in da booth
what was goin down in the beneath
and she jolted out of whatever
self induced reverie... startled...
and hopped on the horn for an S.O.S.
i made my way out the doors
to get to my own turf
(seagulls cryin and waves crashin...
framing my troubled thoughts...
like ghosts in my mental machine...)
i swear i can smell coney island's
ocean air lacing my nostrils
instead of the grit of bed-stuy streets...
and as i slip the key
into the lock of my crib...
i figga i'm home and that i'm safe...
at least that's what i'm choosin to believe
but a part of me cant shake off
this sense of mournin...
like i lost somethin...
or maybe we lost somethin...
and all i can do is
sit in the dark
and silently
weep...

~ :: ~

verse 5

-:¦:-

☠ fuck you ☠

just simply being good ol' "angry me"...

dat shit

this is dat shit
dat shit dat leaves
a bad taste in my mouth
dat shit dat stains
the brain wit
lies, betrayal, denial and hypocrisy
it is dat shit
dat turns my view
from pink to red
wit an anger dat seeps
way down to the marrow
it's dat shit
dat masks concern wit
hidden agendas
when a cry for my help
becomes parasitic
when someone projects
their short comins onto me
it's just dat shit
when cultural community icons
take money from desperate people
from desperate me
leavin false hope
as empty filler
no calories
no nutrients
to sustain the soul
it's dat shit dat
shakes my foundation
knocks me on my ass
havin me scramblin
fightin for a purchase hold
clutchin at my throat
consumin massive gulps of breath
it's dat shit
dat just about makes me forget
that all i had to do
was
let
go
.
.
.

☠

pussy negotiations

I ask you:
How far will you go to negotiate for the pussy?
Telling lies and empty promises seem to be quite easy.
Like a charlatan on yonder corner selling snake oil,
Laying down shaky beginnings for future turmoil.
You're slick like grease that will one day leave a vile stain
And your words of caring are indeed quite profane
As you give promises of colorless rainbows and vacant dreams
While my legs your hands are trying to get in between.

So I ask you again:
How far will you go to negotiate for the pussy?
Will you tell me you love me - then try to hit it and leave me?
Trying to sell yourself to my brothers and to my father -
The challenge is so tempting: that's why you'd even think to bother
If I had children, would you try to act like their special friend?
Cuz you'd think it'll make my sweetness easier to apprehend?
Maybe you'd think I was stupid enough to confuse sex with love
So that you'll have no problems with slipping me on like a glove.

Once more, I ask you:
How far will you go to negotiate for the pussy?
Can you instead just walk away and just leave me be?
Or will you be willing to choke on you own false, empty words
As the bile rises and stabs you repeatedly like a finely honed sword?
Or would you be willing to cross your heart and then proceed to just die
As you pay the high price for perpetuating all those filthy lies?
Or rip out your still pulsing heart and give it to me on a silver platter?
Would you - if you knew that it really and truly mattered?

Uhhh! Too late...
You've hesitated with your reply and I see the fear in your eyes.
Cuz the look that's etched onto my face is the look of despise.
Trying to step to me with those greasy ole slick pimp daddy ways,
Not realizing til it's too late that it's yourself you have played.
Now we both see how far you'll go to negotiate for the "snatch" - -
Til my foot ends up in ya ass and must be surgically detached!

☠

fuck "i love you"

Him: "I love you."

Her: "No you don't. How can you love me when we just got through fucking? No, we damn sure weren't making love. Making love goes deeper than physical penetration. It penetrates the soul and the spirit. Baby, making love is hyperphysical. But this...act that we've committed...this ain't spiritual, baby. It's just FUCKING. I don't understand how you could've made this stupendously stupid bold ass leap from 'fucking' to 'love' when we both had intentions of acting out our lusts. Don't you remember how we looked at each other on the 5^{20} train coming back from the city? You had that 'Maybe the pussy is free' look in your eyes. And I had that 'Maybe the dick is good' look in my eyes. Neither one of us was interested in knowing each others likes and dislikes and various other forms of idiosyncratic behaviors. We just wanted to jump each others bones, roll in the haystack, hit the skins, slap some meat. We didn't want to know each others personal struggles -- like what made you fall to your knees and cry the other day or why was I having severe anxiety attacks. No...no, baby...we just wanted to have some noncommittal sex. And when all the thrusting and moaning and panting and licking and sucking is done, you whispered in my ear the last fucking thing that needed to be said -- 'I love you'. Who do you take me for? Is that what you thought I wanted to hear? Did you feel that you owed me those sacred words backed by hollow meaning? I would've had more respect for you if ya kept it real and said, 'I fuck you'. Then I would have responded back, 'I fuck you too, darling.'"

☠

77

callin muthafuckas out

i'm callin muthafuckas out,
so cease the bullshit
when my presence enters
like the *dragon*.
tolerance is at an all time low.
saturation point has been saturated.
the crapper's full and there's an over flow
so, "Shields up, Captain - - it's about to blow!"
cuz i'm callin muthafuckas out.
talk your rat trap crap
but not behind my back.
can ya face this Medusa?
fearful that your words would freeze
in the craw of your neck,
where you'll choke
on verbalistic bile?
a weak man - - or a weak woman

couldn't even think to RISE
to this challenge.
i may be - at times - meek,
but don't miss and take that as being weak.
"Stupid Asshole Bitch" ain't tattooed
on this lovely forehead
beneath the spiritual crown
bestowed upon my brow.
god may be merciful when it fits,
but even the creator didn't have to take no sh...
no...no! muthafuckas - -
i'm callin ya all out!
fashion terrorists and
3rd party ventriloquists and
sanctified niggers and
snakes with itchy dick triggers and
snobby snooties and
busted cooters with cooties and
pseudo gigolos and
withered up, dirty old ho's and
impostors posing as poets and
flatulaters who think they know it - -
All Ya Muthafuckas -------- OUT!
cuz if ya don't exit
the perimeter of my sight -
i'm gonna whip those pathetic, saggy asses
in front of all of the masses
with words that cut like hot knife through butter
the pain itself will leave ya with a stutter.
so watch what ya read and listen to.
watch your back as well as your front.
ya might get yoked by the clothesline
that's airing out YOUR dirty laundry.
so get OUT, muthafuckas - -
THE EXORCISMS BEGINS!

☠

phoenix

your shit is whack
as you try to elevate yourself
by stepping on the backs of others.
your claws grinding flesh and bone.
but you will fall when i rise
and shake you from my back.
and when i rise,
it will be by the strength
of my will and convictions.
not only will you be scorned,
but you will be scorched
like ashen remains
for all the pain
during the tyranny of your reign.
the higher i rise,
the greater is your downfall.
i am the Phoenix that rises from the flames.
baptism by fire.
don't fuck with me!

4QA

Your desperation ain't my motivation.
Your pleading,
guilt tripping and emotional blackmail
won't move me from my throne.
I've decided for my own good
that I can't allow your needs
to encroach my movements,
molding me into your indentured servant,
leaving me scrambling and scraping
for scraps of time
to handle my own business...
Falling short,
feeling frustrated,
confused and wondering,
"Why?"
I'm passive-aggressive
so it's imperative for me to speak out,
to no longer internalize
my growing resentment of you.
I can no longer bring harm to my Self.
I shall no longer poison my essence
with toxic thoughts.
Not with such a lack of respect
can you expect me to be part of your madness.
And you offer no apologies
for such trespasses of the spirit.
So I would be a fool
to abandon my life for your needs.
Amidst the chaos you have brought to my door,
I stood in the center of my soul.
Physical eyes shut, palms up and First Eye watching.
The answer I have blessed you with in the beginning
remains the same.
Its repetitive utterance
maintains my balance and focus.
"NO."
Your desperation ain't my motivation.

☠

hypocrites

hypocrites with crippling thoughts creeping on the edge of oblivion, wearing masks of deception well worn like an old pair of faded jeans which is only shed in the shadows of the night whenever the moon is at its blackest and everyone sleeps the deepest at the same moment of time. hypocrites dance the wild dance of lies, intermingled with some truth to gain trust, combined into grey issues that creates whole lies. they wear the clothes of those that you would think should know better... and they do know better. but they choose to use their powers for evil instead of good. they will fight you word for word, wu-tang style and justify all and every transgression with a smoothed forked tongue and the slight of hand. they make lawyers look like saints and politicians look like rank amateurs. they come in many shapes, colors, sizes and backgrounds... but they all are from the same steelo: low energy psychic vampyrs sucking you dry to the bone. and if you close your eyes and trust in you, you can feel them a mile away, nervous little mites wondering how long it is before their cover is cold stone blown from tripping over their own fraud. they would then be force to hide like roaches before the spiritual raid begins to kick their asses. but they do have their place in the universe... just like ticks, fleas, leeches, tapeworms... you get the idea.

☠

ex - case and point

i kept it casual
while u looked for every angle
to bogart ur way back into my life
implorin that u need to see me
like there was no choice
                but ur need was just an illusion
alludin to the last chance to finally control
the "one that got away"
u bring to the table neither
intellectual nourishment nor sensitivity
aint no "we" in ur speak
just u
and ur desire to subjugate me at last
afta all these years...
or so u thought
all of this began to surface
only after day 3
of speakin on the phone with u
and mind u, before that,
we aint seen each other in over 13 years
like a professional matador
i side-step ur calls
and i hear
ur frothin frustration leakin
in the form of hardly contained
condescendin tones
in ur converse
dictatin the terms of how we should interact
based on some distorted
male/female stereotypical role-play in ur head
hostility barely masked
by the forced lightness of ur voice
                domination
                obsession
                compulsion
                        to capture
                        to break
                        to conquer
as u leave
            back 2
                    back 2
                            back 2
                                    back
messages in the bottles
of my voicemail...

i hit multiples 7s to delete –
tappin out the morse code for
"naw mufucka, i aint callin u back!"
aint in my job description
in the first place
to explain why i refuse to pick up the phone...
i see u still got that
self-sensory deprivation shit goin on:
u aint tryin to see...
u aint tryin to hear...
u aint tryin to feel...
how ur persistence is cra-zee stalkerishly creepy
to begin and end with

that no matter what i say
u will do ur damndest to try convince me otherwise
cuz u already orchestrated the
"once upon a time" and "the happily ever after"
in the tracks of ur mental
to reconnect aint got shit to do with
u tryin to noose my neck
so that ur grip wont slip this time around
but peep this...
im hip to ur slick lip
more so now than when i was 16
and as i dip
my spirit rips
away
ur psychotic bullshit
u aint neva gonna be ready for the woman ive become
because u cant handle my truth
this time around
it took 3 days
instead of 3 years
but i wish it took only 3 seconds...
see, there are reasons why
an ex is an ex
and should stay an ex
neva to be considered even for friendship
and u are the poster-child for the cause
case and point

☠

48 hour ultimatum

ultimatums bring
ultimate ulcers to the mind...
lacerated thoughts
barbed and flung far
to ensnare and snag
the tongue's tonality
until your victims becomes
tone deaf and brainwashed
into praying for the death
of hedonistic self-liberation.
i dance not
to your demands...
i defy the prissiness of your prude...
you fight to preserve
pristine missionary positional illusions
while i freak nasty
my sexual jism
all over this page...
you can't hold the floodgates
of delusional denial forever...
not even for 48 fuckin hours...
the gall is so gargantuan...
incredulous, even...
but i am your reality checker...
leaning over to whisper
those magical free-thinking words...
"wake up..."
and when you at long last do,
you finally notice
the dust settling around your ankles
after this melee is way over...
maybe next time,
you will quicker come to grip
with the fact that...
ultimatums bring
ultimate ulcers to *your* mind...
and that *you* will finally cease
harming *your* Self
and put an end to attempting
to shut down others
because of your own
self imposed restraints...

game over

it is pretty liberating for me
to say it and mean it...
the freedom to let go
supersedes most of the
hurt and disappointment
maneuvering me
into a position where
i can clearly see
that i would be better off
no longer dealing with you...
saying it is so much
easier when all your shit
is finally gone from my house...
that towel you left behind...
your digital camera
with those dead ass batteries...
and a couple of nick-nacks
that were no more
than misappropriated
tokens of affection
intermingled with the remnants
of your energy...
all at last depart like
motes and flotsam
caught in the winds of exodus...
these are the things
that you insist diligently
in your sexiest
makeshift billy dee voice,
"but baby, just hold on to them for me.
they ain't gonna take up no space in yo house."
yet, holding on to those things
means holding on to you
which reinforces your hold on me
and i can't let your holding on
fuck up my game plan
just cuz you were never honest
with your own game plan...
so...
game over, bruh...
goodbye...

verse 6

-:-

back bone

this is not about being perfect. perfection is such an illusive imaginary lover. we are talking about the progressive work of Self... a never ending project born out of Love.

the Love of oneself is being accountable and taking a stand for who you are no matter the adversity or the labeling from others. how others see you is of very little importance. how you may actually see yourself when tapping into the higher consciousness of Self, past all the mundane minutia and into something far greater than you've been exposed to in your past, is one of the ultimate goals of existence.

my journey is your journey is our collective journey. it is a lot of work but there are such great rewards, _peace of mind_ being at the forefront, that can not be denied. so set your ego aside and slide into the ride of your mind with no more to hide. claim your higher Self and know you can handle your due... peace unto you...

Who I be?
I be Me...
that She...
my Mama's Legacy.
I be THAT She
who's spirit is flying free
swingin on front porches
with mad, mad rhythms...
talkin bout love, life
& crazy izm-schizms.
I be that She
Tribal Warrior Goddess
of the BellyFeast
steppin Bed-Stuy completion
from west to east.
three hundred & sixty hot full-tation
1st Eye scopin all these nations
birthed from My Wombniverse,
the cradle of civilizations.

followin Paths of Divinity &
Rebirthed by a Hyperphysical means
I be that She...
Mama, Sistah, Queen, & Lover...
Priestess, Madonna, Healer & Creator
so ask Me again...
who I be?
I be Me
I be She
I be of We
~ :: ~

meditation of self

flipping scripts
making minds trip
causing me to sit
and chant "A N K H"
in meditation
as I analyze ramifications
of actions taken
without thought
or consideration.
reflection is the perfection
of the mind, body & soul –
mending spiritual holes
making one whole –
completion...
with deletions
of otherness
to encompass the Oneness
of Being.
I can peep what I am seeing –
with physical eyes closed,
primary eye open!
the essence is smokin
before burning up,
then blowing up
into the realization of
Higher Consciousness.
forget that conventional mess.
that's for the weak.
strength is the protocol
for this call
of the Spirit.
I can hear it.
past the trees
for the forest
into the furthest reaches
of the cranium –
the stadium
of the thought medium.

ascension begins with ⇦in Self,
not with⇨out Self.
for Self is the beginning
of the Universe
with the first utterance of
"A N K H"
life.
no strife,
stress or
worry.
no anger,
regrets or
hurry.
just reflection
of past mistakes to
mend the present and
secure the future,
creating a strong foundation
through revelations
brought into being by meditations.
I dive in and delve deeply
into my psyche
and take note of what
my Spirit sees.
a glowing ember
of being
surrounded by the darkness
of the Wombniverse.
presence begins at conception,
that first intention
of thought.
and the One Most High said:
'Let There Be Light!'
and so was the glimmer
that grew
into
I.

~ :: ~

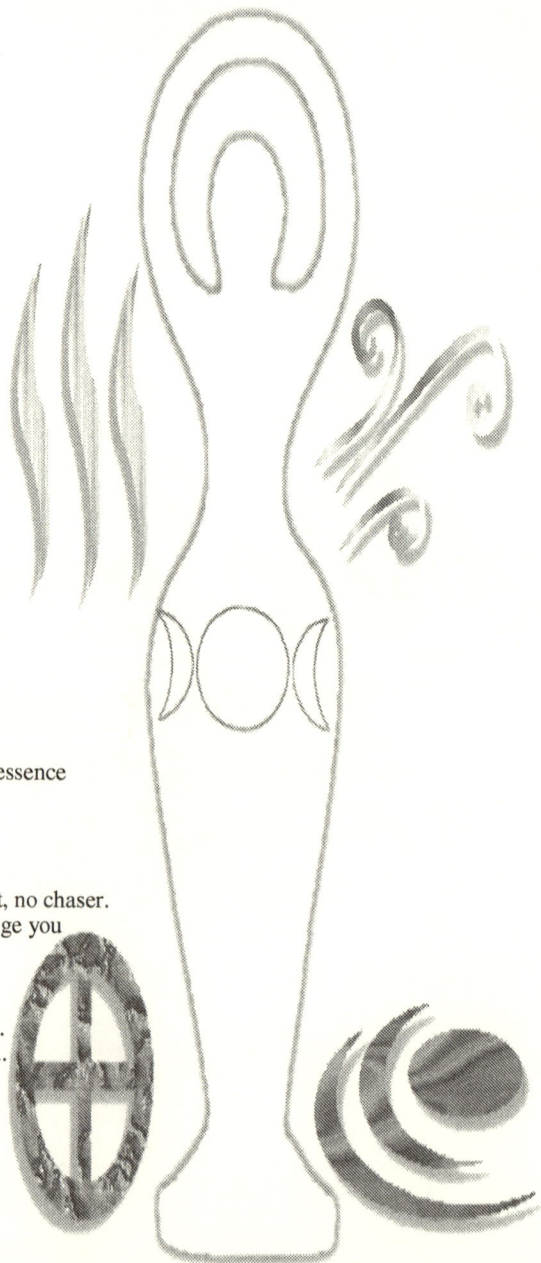

elemental

I Inspire you with my fire.
Burn you with my words.
Verbalistic baptism by the flame.
Outer-dermis flays away
as my heat touches your soul - -
Igniting that spark...
That first mark...
That makes you wanna leap
from the cliffs of anticipation.
Causing wings of determination
to unfurl from your back.
Gonna take you higher!
and Higher!
The breath of my words
batters you like the buffeting winds
and challenges your ascent into the
HEAVENS...
and you rise to that challenge
by reason of my phonetic stimulus
and by reason of your own flames.
I Drown you in my mad metaphors.
Saturate your lungs
with expressed thoughts of freedom,
spoken words of liberation,
poetic proses of real revolution - -
from the strong sister that I am.
cuz true inspiration don't stop...
and can't stop!
I Bury you in my soil of soliloquies.
Brown earth rolls from my tongue
like a bulldozer,
pushing a payload of enriching
fertile thoughts right through
your cranial cavity.
You absorb my vocal nutriments
right down to the fundamental quintessence
of your soul.
It tastes as sweet as maple syrup
on organic pancakes.
That's what I am...
ORGANIC – homegrown ⇨ straight, no chaser.
And yes, sister and brother, i challenge you
to be true to your own
revealing verbal revolutions.
so i burn you with my words...
batter you with my buffeting winds...
drown you with my mad metaphors...
bury you in my soil of soliloquies.
Inspiration comes as it may,
just as it comes in the words
that i say.
It's all
Elemental...

~ :: ~

steppin

i steps - completion
cuz if I ½ step,
i might trip into the trapfalls
that fools trip into -
pitfalls for the pitiful.
backsliding into quagmires
that leaves the mind in dire -
straight and focus is how I travel.
at the speed of light is my flight.
patterns are all I discern -
pictures are worth more than thousands of words...
scope them temple walls
that reveal them ancient secrets...
like the blossoming of the first Lotus
and the initial realization that
immortality and one's spirit
are synonymous with never-ending.
ending never with anger and
abstaining from nonessential rhetoric
for twenty-one days,
i center my focus
and balance it on the apex of eternity -
the eternal merkut.
foundation is infinity... that is times three.
triumvirate - triumphant.
i sense NTRU on the horizon,
where Nut and Geb
join in consecrated matrimony,
blowing brass trumpets.
my love for my divine
is more than sublime.
it is all encompassing.
as it is above, so shall it be below...
left, right, to and fro... my 'fro, my 'fro...
my afro sways like weeping willows
in the wind in the Bayou.
'cept, I'm in Bed-Stuy.
steppin' by, steppin' by...
[oh shit! I just crushed that roach!]
not tryin' to get high outside of me.
just tryin' to get by.
so don't even think to knock me down...
i said, don't even think to knock me down.
cuz I walked sentinel - guarded and protected.
ill will I have detected and deflected.
cuz all I ever wanted was a little...Ah-men.
cuz all I ever wanted was a little...Aśe.
cuz all I ever wanted was a little...Hotep.
so completion is my step to my inner peace.

~ •• ~

93

pandora's locks

I got an earache from all the sweet talk
you be tryin to give me.
Tryin to lull me off my guard with the
curve of your masculine lips
and that glint of a gleam
off your eye tooth
that matches the gleam
in your soft brown eyes...
as you lean over and in your
most sultry bedtime voice,
you ½ whispered in my ear:
"Yo... Sista, I'm diggin ya locks."
Oh yes, the finesse of your
fine-ness was not denied unto you
and I suppose the attention
that you paid in full
to my physical was
a compliment – of sorts.
I should have felt grateful
for the attention that you
graced me with... but...
...Do you know who I am?
Really now...
I am the entity known as SHE.
Other halves of better
I do not seek
cuz I breathe in completion
and surround myself
with mirrored beings that
directly reflect the multitude
of my existence.
I am SHE –
Nüt of the Heavens.
From my breasts drips
the milky way of the Wombniverse.
My belly pregnant with
future generations.
My mind is creations ahead
of the last idea I bore
into fruition
as righteous fruits of labor
falls from my womanly Haven.
Come seek refuge in my shadow
and you will not be denied.
Cuz as you step through
my astral threshold,
flesh and blood and bone shall
be flayed away to
lay bare solely the fire
of your spirit.
And I will nurture your flame

for fire is a purification
of your soul.
From my navel extends
the mystical umbilical cord of life.
Please, take hold so that you may
find strength to grapple
with your lower existence
and succeed in the battles
of Self versus Ego.
Cuz whether you acknowledge
or not, I have peeped you with my
axiomatic oculus as you
stepped to me with your
inflated Ego and depleted Self
and I can not condone the
imbalance of those scales
within in the perimeter of my person.
I utter harmonic scales –
the Music of the Spheres –
{AAANNNKKKHHH!!!}
Motion of molecules
known as vibration from
chants of meditation
that shakes loose the
filthy entrapments of self
mummification.
I notice you flinch from
the touch of my sound.
Don't be afraid.
I only show you the Glory.
One should always be
prepared to behold
the beauty of the Lotus
if that one is so willing
to touch its petals.
And brother you have opened
this Pandora's box
when you whispered
the key in my ear.
You put the shovel
to the ground,
diggin my locks.
You unearthed
ancient buried fortunes.
So I must ask you two Questions:
Why should you fear
the awareness of your discovery?
&
Why should you fear
the discovery of your own awareness?

~ :: ~

Sometimes a single mama's job can be a thankless and unappreciative role. After all the blood, sweat and tears, after all the sleepless nights of dealing with a high grade fever brought on by a recurring ear infection, after scrounging for change around the house to buy your child food for the week, the last thing that your challenged and slightly bruised spirit was prepared to hear was, "Daddy's the greatest!"

And, of course, the walls of the dam begin to crack because you're wondering where's your acknowledgement from your own child for all the times that you were there when she needed you? Where is the credit for all your energy pulled from God-knows-where to keep a roof over his head, food in her belly, and clothes on his back? How dare she place her no-show daddy on a pedestal just because, for the first time in three months, he's taking her for one lousy, stinking weekend?!

The truth is children are so grateful for the little time they get from their nearly absent father, they are willing to shout their happiness to the high heavens regardless of how it rubs Mama's bruised ego and raw emotions. Their thoughts and perceptions are idealistic. Until they are conditioned otherwise, children are innocent dreamers. For them, life is perfect despite the imperfections around them.

Of course, some fathers live with the thought, whether they are present or not, that they can go about their business knowing their children will always be taken care of. Mamas, for the most part, are nurturers. No mama in her right mind would like to see her child be without food, clothes and shelter. Despite all her hard work, in Mama's eyes, Peek-a-Boo Papa seems to get all the love from the children. And why not when he will do things to compensate for the all the no-shows? Like taking the children to the movies or shopping at the mall. The rules are more relaxed around Peek-a-Boo Papa. Check out the cell phone he just gave his teenage daughter! Hell, being with Papa is like Christmas for the day.

Notice I said, "for the day". Because as the evening draws to a close and right before the kids night time grumpiness kicks in, they are back with Mama. No welcome is worn out between Papa and the kids. So this title of the "Greatest" hasn't been tarnished by any confrontations or challenges. But let him be with his darling angels for longer than 12 to 24 hours... how about for a week or two? He will swear they had sprouted horns, and have been birthed from the loins of Lucifer himself.

However, just because Mama is not getting her just-deserved kudos from her own child does not give her the right to smash her child's dreams by telling her child how no good Peek-a-Boo Papa is. Children really don't want to hear or believe either one of their parents is a terrible person. Children need both of their parents regardless of what issues the parents have not resolved between themselves. The issues Mama has with Peek-a-Boo Papa really have nothing to do with the children's relationship with their father. A lot of these issues existed pretty much before pregnancy – overlooked, ignored, denied and unresolved – surfacing to the top to raise their ugly heads at a time when you're still not ready to deal with them.

One of the most damaging things Mama can do to the relationship she has with her children is either argue with or bad mouth their Papa in front of the children. This kind of explosive emotional behavior places the children in a precarious position of having to choose one over the other out of loyalty or hating both parents all together or feeling that it's their fault their parents are at such odds. Especially when the children are young and can barely understand the complexities of life in general. There is nothing wrong with Mama being honest with her children when they're asking about their papa or her relationship with him but it is important to speak the truth with as much balance as possible. Children don't often understand the underlying resentment Mama feels for Papa. All they understand is that Mama holds down the fort and Papa gives all the treats. Stability and fun.

So Mama, please don't use the truth to shut your children down just because they seem to be giving Peek-a-Boo Papa more love than they're giving you. Don't get pissed when your children want to give him their love. After all, the love they give to him is the love you showed them how to give. How well your children come out is the validation of your hard work and love. When your children grow up without drug problems, when your children escape teenage pregnancy, when your children go to college, when your children want you to take them fishing, when your infant child greets you with a big old smile in the morning, when your child wants you to come to the school play, you have been given your acknowledgement.

Because we Mamas are the ones dealing with the day-to-day business nurturing them, we can lose sight of the many signs of love our children give us. It doesn't make us bad mamas. We're just too caught up in the day-to-day with no one to rub our backs or feet when the children are finally asleep. We get frustrated and a little bitter around the edges. Thus, we are ready to explode.

Personally, as a single Mama, how well my own son turns out is a huge validation for me. I'm working hard to make sure he has the tools necessary to be a better person and to grow from both his own mistakes and from his parents' mistakes as well. So when I feel the world closing in, when I feel frustrated at his father, when I think there's nothing the world can offer me to make things the way I always wanted them to be, I grab up my son, run to the bathroom mirror and say, "Who's that beautiful Mama holding that beautiful Baby Boy?" And my heart is a whole lot lighter when I see those big kool-aid grins reflecting back at us. This is when I know that I am the greatest in my son's eyes!

~ :: ~

iowan's return

anger
bitterness
sadness
regret
stress
flowed thru my veins
molten lava
a volcano newly erupted
life disrupted
4 years
thrown back
in2 my face
how have i
kept the pace
...back then
my son came
2 weeks past due
after the day
he finally admitted
he had no desire
4 me
i, who carried his seed
thus my world stopped
my labor stopped
stressed out
the veil ascended
the true pain began
love/hate
same coin
flip sides
conflicting emotions
rushed me like
tsunami linebackers
couldn't catch my breath
...my thoughts
...my spirit
...my self
2 proud 2 die
2 broken 2 go forward
just stuck
but suddenly
i came thru the void
1 of the worst chapters
in my life's book
now behind me
the pain just suddenly

seem to cease...
but it was really
a gradual ease
over time... 4 myself
over distance... from him
... from the situation
... from everybody else
and yet still
putting more distance
from him
obtaining emotional detachment
2 regain focus
to see
what really matters
calling upon
my spirit
4 drama exorcism
unsheathing my
ritual dragon dagger
cutting away
dead weighted issues
exposing darkness
bringing enlightenment
using my inner tarot
reading my situation
and
scrying my mind
4 answers
from the ancestors
working that mojo
4 myself
2 demand better
from myself
and
from those around me
in order 2 be
intact
satisfied
relaxed
realized
i no longer hate
not even angry
i have forgiven myself
i can go forward again
i am
moving on

~ :: ~

being air

some might say i'm flighty
when in fact, my mind's a flight risk
thoughts are by leaps and bounds
with none of the ties that bind
it's just that aquarius shit, being air

babblin cuz lips fight to keep up with thoughts
words tumblin down like tower of babel
multi-tongue slobberin poly-syllabique verbage
rapid fire sound assault for the senses
it's just that aquarius shit, being air

i care... sometimes too much..
the givin of myself until there is nothin left for myself
wishin to heal the universe with just one kiss
or to save a soul with a touch of laughter
it's just that aquarius shit, being air

i embody the nearly forgotten qualities of youthfulness
a childlike playfulness not easily grasped by others
i really don't find it very difficult to fly
and live life's experience with a consistent renewal of faith
it's just that aquarius shit, being air

lovin hard and lovin strong
the passion that fuels the flame
gettin open, bein open, and stayin open
caught on fire, burnin brightly, never extinguished
it's just that aquarius shit, being air

~ :: ~

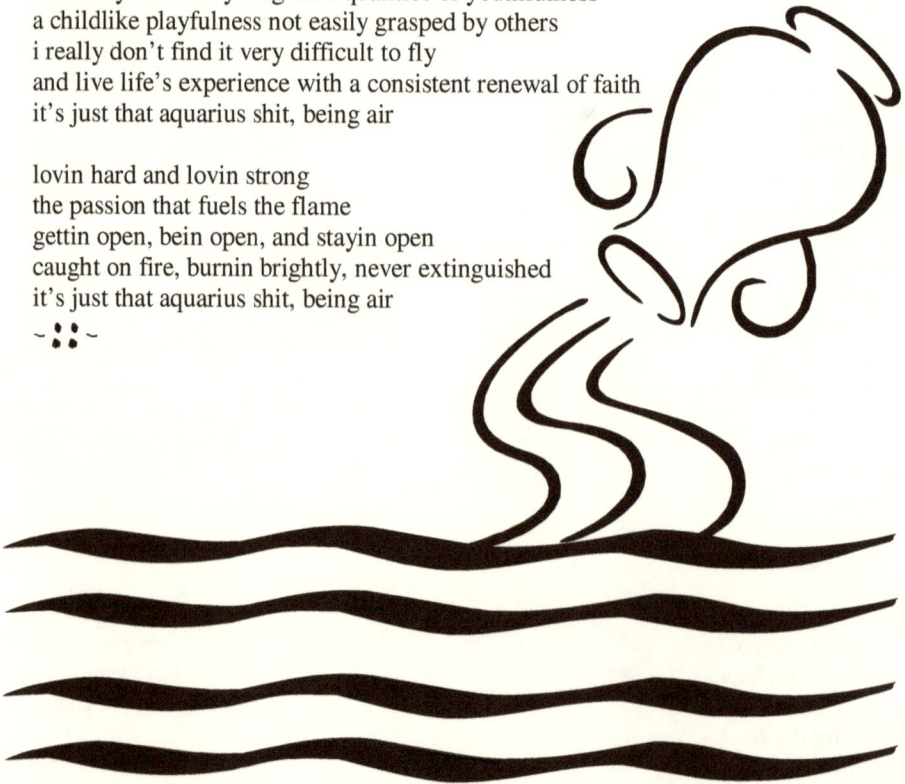

rain

never realized how cleansing
rain can be...until i find
myself caught up in its
downpour - a deluge and torrential -
where chinatown ends
and tribeca begins
off of canal street.
washing away all the
silt and soot and crap
abandoned on black streets
by fingers that do indeed care less.
black streets that covers earth mama's
earth brown skin -
urbanized suffocation...
urbanized suffocation...
urbanized suffocation.
but the creeping of encroaching civilization
can not stop earth mama's elixir -
the primary drink of the goddesses...
rain, downpour - a deluge and torrential -
replenishes her strength and
fortifies her patience and
cleanses her spirit...
replenishes her strength and
fortifies her patience and
cleanses her spirit...
so she laughs and i feel
her mirthful rumblings
through the soles of my feet
and through the soul of my spirit
as she sips through the cracks and
fissures of urbanized suffocation -
fractures and flaws in the
bound shackle known as pavement.
she laughs for she is biding time
and time is her finely honed weapon,
reinforced by the primary elixir -
rain, downpour - a deluge and torrential.
so in honor of her revelations,
I cast my umbrella aside
and tilt my head to the heavens...
arms open to receive and
eyes open to witness and
mouth open to drink
the primary elixir of the goddesses,
for am i not a goddess?
do i not share this affinity
with my sister, earth mama, as well?
so together, earth mama and i
share in the secret of true power-
rain, downpour - a deluge and torrential
and i drown in its cleansing touch.

~ :: ~

love's free verse

ive perceived men to be dirty
self-servin creatures...
bereft of sensitivity...
emotionally inept

makin it easy to vilify them
whenever my intimacies have failed...
makin it easy to hate them
instead of doin tha work
to understand tha intricacies of their issues
in order for me to see
tha reflection of my own issues within them.

i confess this cuz
i aint tryin to be a slave to this sickness...
this pain and disappointment perpetuated.
im thinkin that one day
when i achieve a deeper understandin,
i will find myself able to write love poems
minus tha hypocrisy,
wit a couple of measures of heart and honesty...

strong death defyin love poems
that resurrect tha dearly departed
and wash away tha sins of a society psychotic
hell bent on tha indoctrination of self hate.

love poems that can keep papa from bein a rollin stone
so his son dont have to hustle to make that money flow
makin desperate attempts to buy his way out of abandonment

love poems that keep a woman from slittin her wrists
cuz tha world dont feel her tha way she wanna be felt...
dont hear her tha way she wanna be heard...
dont see her tha way she wanna be seen

love poems that make christian women challenge tha church
and demand to see them missin pages torn from tha bible
that spoke so openly of
female prophets, preachers, avatars and saints
you know... them backbone women
like corretta and betty and nina and ella and my moms, yo

love poems powerful enuf
to make ya realize that it wasnt your fault
you were raped and beaten and brutalized,
my sistah... and my brutha...

love poems so sturdy
that your daily death wish ceased to exist,
addictions no longer afflicted your soul
like riddlin bullet holes up and down your body
and your scars miraculously disappear
like nightmares burned away by tha sun.

love poems that keep a broke up woman
from makin her only son
her man replacement
and keep a tore down man
from makin his only daughter
his stand in wife.

love poems that will make a man realize
that when he call women bitches
its cuz his mama wasnt there for him
when he was a little boy like he wanted her to be.

love poems that will make sisters
stop fightin each other over pieces of a man...
table scraps if you will...
and focus on buildin the self-esteem
to prepare for a true banquet
of queen goddess adoration

love poems that keep a man from losin his mind
and constantly gettin jacked by pussy
cuz he confusin sex wit love wit fuckin
fuckin around wit sex
fuckin around wit love
just fuckin around...

love poems that will make a nation realize
that nigger aint a badge...
its a gotdam burden
still branded over the collective first eye,
blockin higher vision...

you know... them kinda love poems
i dont wanna miss out on
not in this life time
so im thinkin that one day
when i do achieve a deeper understandin,
i will find myself able to write those love poems
its jus a matta of time...

~ :: ~

verse 7

~:!:~

mystic luv

the tickling of the fancy. the tantalizing of the taste. the hint of desire on the edges of pheremonic feelings. seeing the possibilities of bodily contours. discreet whispers of new promises uttered to the four directions of love. what are the first sparks that will hopefully lead to forever passion? because love for another is such a powerful force, it is so beyond human control and it can often intimidate you as it embraces your five senses into the budding of the awareness of another.

though there are no guarantees where this may lead, that first flush will always leave you wide open and alive and eternally hopeful for a new and fulfilling encounter. just follow the glow of the flow...

your voice...

The sound
of your voice,
the epitome of
masculinity
rich with the flavors
of baritones
vibrating
from my ears,
down the length
of my neck,
through the cavity
of my chest
where it stays...
but a bit,
playing
resonance with my heart
as it wraps itself
like gossamer threads
and gently,
ever
so gently
pulse
with my life beat
and continues on
through the warmth
of my belly,
into my womanhood
where it
freely speaks true
of a promise of many nights
together.

~ **:** ~

heartbeat's 1st kiss

Heart beat
You make me feel so weak.
Heart beat
You make me feel so weak.
Heart beat
You make me feel so weak.

-Tanya Gardner

Spring time.

A gentle breeze blows.

I can hear its sweet caress through the blades of grass and the rustling green tree leaves.

The air smells fresh.

I can hear the melodic, dulcet warbling of sparrows and cardinals and occasional defiant screeches of blue jays and crows.

It is lunch time as I and the boy of my heart walk across the high school football field to the bleachers where I would nestle comfortably in the strength of his arms as we talk about whatever girlfriends and boyfriends talk about.

We have never kissed before. Or I should say that I, at age 16, have never kissed before. The thought of warm lips touching, of tongues committing acts of intimacy invoke such intense feelings within myself that I'm fascinated as well as intimidated by the idea.

That was why whenever he did want us to reach this tableau of physical intimacy, I shied from the idea. I'm in no rush cuz I'm not sure if I could handle the kiss itself or whatever it may unleash within me.

However, there was no side stepping his request today. The forces of Nature was playing against my strength of will along with his gentle cajoling as the slight lisp in his speech pattern tickled my ear. "Baby, don't you wanna know what it feels like? Don't you wanna try it?"

And I hesitated with my reply. Damn. Usually I would flat out tell him I was not ready but...it sure was a good day to try something new.

Without waiting for a verbal reply, he brings me closer to him, tilting his head a little to the right and I, being new to this whole idea, tilt my head to my right, mimicking him. No need to bump noses or any of that nonsense.

When it finally happens, him covering my mouth with his own, my tongue playing hide and seek with his, shortly that little game ends as I quickly figure out how the mechanics of the situation works. It was not too long when I started getting creative.

Meanwhile, I was receiving the most interesting sensations as my body responded in its own unique way. Boogie electric dancing on my insides - backflips and spins and what not.

I realized that this was a very very very good feeling. Very exciting. Yes! I could like this groove!

106

Here I was with a boy that at one time I wanted so much that I ached. We were friends but I would usually have vicious mood swings because I was so angry at the thought of him going out with other girls.

There were times he did not know whether to approach me or not. But one day he figured out what it was that I had trouble verbalizing and we started "going together" after that.

Which brings me back upon the reflection of that first kiss upon the bleachers in the high school football field as the sun shined and the breeze blew and the birds chirped.

Could it have felt more magical than that?

I did not think it could. And really, there will never be another wondrous sensation as that first kiss.

"You're suppose to close your eyes. Why are you kissing with your eyes opened?" He asked and I could hear the slight irritation in his voice.

I pulled back away from him, a little shocked. "Why should I close my eyes? It doesn't serve a purpose. I want to see you."

"You're suppose to fantasize while you're kissing. It makes it more exciting," he replied.

"But, baby aren't you good enough?"

And he looks at me funny. He just doesn't get it.

~ :: ~

the embrace

he celebrates
the roundness of me
kneeling at my feet
holding steady like
rock solid foundation
one arm encircling
the swerve of my hips &
the curve of my backside
one hand resting
on the softness of my belly
the warmth of his countenance
connecting to my vessel
listening to future's secrets
yet untold &
smiling at
privilege ancient information

~ :: ~

eyes

eyes need not be open to feel.
best feelings come as waves
that wash over your being.
sometimes as gentle as a baby's
breath...
sometimes as heavy as a tsunami...
the only consistency –
eyes need not be open to just feel.
eyes can not accurately describe
1,000 fluttering wings of
500 monarch butterflies
in a spring full of a field of daisies.
there is no apt description of
love's first, profound kiss.

~ :: ~

brash

Brash, limber –young energy on the verge of surety in regards to your manhood.
Around your peers, you are callow and new-sprung.
But when you are alone, there is a steely calm that defies description as you count the bars of silent measures in your life's aria.
Calculating and decisive.
Yes, I feel you burn holes through my tangible self – into my inner.
Like a deer caught in the headlights, my essence stood stock-still.
I catch my breath.
Recognition...
Gasping.
I think our spirits met...or perhaps it was the Eastern wind on the nape of my neck.
No, it was the heat of your peppery breath.
Hot, spicy, pungent.
I swelter at the thought of your technique.
Could I, too, bring you to burn like I?
Perhaps you are giving to me what I already have given to you – unseen yet felt on an alternate plane of existence – we took it to a more elevated level.
When I turn around to face you, I find that you are physically far across the room from I, – (but the breath of your spirit has touched my soul...) – your eyes dancing with roguish mirth.
Who do we feel, but each other?
I will never divulge this rudimentary secret and, from the hidden look on your bronze burnished face, neither will you.
For knowledge is power and this shared knowing is our power together.
For you, being young is not a hindrance. You are but a returning Ancestor.
You blinked in your Previous Life and opened your eyes in this Now Life in a fresh new vessel called Young King.

~:!:~

she had a scar under her eye,
right at the crease
and no one would ever noticed it
unless she was being madeloveto
or when she was being watched
as she slept
he was privileged
to bear witness to that
near hidden blemish
it spoke of perfection
within the imperfection
and each time he saw it
it reminded him of
her proximity to his body
the scent of coconut mango
upon her melanated skin
and the aroma of
nature's blessings entwined
in the coils of her
macrobiotic mane
late at night, after an
arousal game of
cherished play
he would lay awake
and watch as she slept
fearful that he would miss
some small detail of her
that he must record
in his melanin memory
the rhythm of her breath
the pattern that her mane
created on their pillow
the sleepingdancepose
of her slumbering form
love was not enough
to capture how he felt
about their union
there was no way
to capture freedom

and insult it with
cheap labels inundated
with mundane clichés
there was only being
and becoming
and coming together
two totalities creating
an elevated union…
a divine coalescence
divisible by no lower forces
multiplied by abundant blessings
so when he finally
succumb to the
warmth of sleep
the strength of the union
filled his dreams
until the images became
visions foretelling of
of their unlimited
potential in and around
their life's bond
"legacy" is what it whispered
to him each time his eyes
met hers in this
otherworld of reverie
the intensity of awareness
caused him to wake with
a start back into this world
back to coconut mango
and nature's blessings
filling his nostrils
but now he has laid witness
to the task that would be
put before the both of them
a journey, a path,
perhaps even a mission
the heritage that must be
maintained through their union

~ :: ~

reach

he sat on the edge of his bed, enveloped in the sudden silence between them that spoke volumes of awareness. he just wanted to kiss her. just grab her up and kiss her savagely upon her well defined lips and down her neck to taste the sweet and salt of her softness. he desired to smooth back the wild, untamed, sexy kinks from around her honey brown face so that he can drown unconditionally in the peacefulness of her eyes. he wanted to press upon her so tight that there would be no space between them... that they would fit like the only two pieces to life's puzzle. he wanted to... he wanted... so as she got up to leave, he reached out, gently grabbed her by the hand and said...

she had the undying urge to discover the answer to his enigma. to experience that new feeling with gentle unfamiliar touches, strokes and caresses. the study of his expressions. the feel of his brown texture beneath her fingertips. she wanted to endure the masculinity of his face, the laughter around his eyes, the deep thoughts that creased his forehead and the mirth that danced on his well formed lips. so as she sat cross-legged next to him on his bed, she felt almost ashamed from the sudden awareness of these urges for they had been only friends and now... so as she stood up to leave, she felt him gently grab her by the hand and heard him say...

"don't go."
>   ...and at these two words, their eyes met and they realized.

~ :: ~

smilin

ridin iron horses twice a day...
five outta da week...
got me reflectin as i'm tunnellin...
about above ground activities
to commit in autumnal times
reflectin red, orange, brown & gold shades
of my spirit.
brisk wind skims my cranium
where thoughts are conceived
& harbored
for personal satisfaction & safe keepin.
some quite naive in conjecture & others...
well...
illicit could aptly describe
why they encourage
knowinly dark & exquisite
smiles in my eyes.
autumn is the occasion of letin go,
just as them trees surrender their leaves
as offerins to the ebb & flow
of the forces of time.
exposin bare branches,
encouragin me
to further bare my soul
for the whole universe to experience...
& damnation to those
who flinch from the battle scars
i've acquired along my arduous
but rewardin journey.
them scars
have shaped me
into the goddess
you see before you.
for each pain i've endured,
a lesser self had crumbled away
only to be replaced by a higher,
stronger self
in
love.
it is a blessin to be a woman,
to not be intimidated
by my own greatness by virtue
&, above all else,
to love every aspect
& crevice of who i am.

to relish in the power
of my every thought, word & touch.
to know there is nothin absolutely wrong
with lovin someone strongly, softly, secretly & out loud.
so i stand before you naked & open.
feelin the rhythms of your dance
echo in my soul
as drums beat staccato tempos
in the ethers.
a pride of lions are your movements -
motion smooth,
pourin across the city's tundra,
takin my spirit beyond boundaries,
past mundane survival.
fluid movements
flowin like cool indigo lava
saturatin my core.
& to watch you dance
as gems of sweat
trickle down your face, neck, back
& other bodily contours
i realize that i am watchin creation
at its best
thus my inner thighs
become slick
with the wet...
hot...
sticky...
sweetness...
of my flavor.
your
presence
i
savor.

~ :: ~

fussin

u fussin at me...
fusin
unique
sensual
syncopated
intellectuality
nocturnally
in my auditory canal...
& im jus eatin it up
like it wuz tha lass supper
like u be christ like
like i be disciple like
takin notations
of the tonal qualities
of ur voice box...
rhythmical bass line rumblins
& a hint of that
concrete & steel street twang
at the core of ur thought processes...
(now thass some gansta shit)
proceedin to turn me on
like g.e. light bulbs
signifyin
ideas & plans
in the grander scheme
of the one universal aria
thoughts excite me
speakin jacks me
sharin comforts me
brutha, u jus dont know
how i relish every syllable u express
& i be real stingy
with ur speak...
like im in a darkened room...
the curtains drawn...
the door bolted shut...
& me in my nakedness...
exposed & open...
(beyond vulnerable)
to the elements
of ur syntactical dexterity
it be that type of shit...
even when yo ass be fussin at me...
um...yeah...

~ :: ~

ponder

sometimes i wonder
if connections are
just my imagination
or just an illusion
that lead to allusions
and assumptions of character...
but then i realize that
it's my insecurity
trying to sneak up on me
and bushwhack me
with doubt and 2nd guessing

i respond to that
deeper part of you
past the potential
and straight to the core
of who you really be...
naked and stripped
of ego and bravado
and how you believe
people should see you...
right down to who
you really are
when no one is looking

i observe these things
because that is who i am
deep down inside
and it fuels my compassion
and understanding
and patience
and love...
in its truest sense

i am compelled
to feel you
to see you
to speak... you...

otherwise
i would be
lying and dishonoring
who i am...
deep down inside...

~ :: ~

verse 8

~ :: ~

soft... wet... black sweat...

this here is grown folk bizness... put them kids to bed, pour yourself a goblet of ambrosia, put on some barry white, turn down the lights...

and

just

feel

me...

feeling sex : feeling you

i feel like sex...
i feel like submerging my body into a tub of warm scented water
and laying there soaking in its softness as i think about you.

i feel like sex...
i feel like listening to a funky instrumental that takes my mind on a ride
through the clouds while the orgasmic organ strokes as i think about you.

i feel like sex...
i feel like swiveling my hips and jumping up and spinning around
and caressing my entire body while i dance as i think about you.

i feel like sex...
i feel like laying naked in my bed enshroud in night's eboned cloak
with the windows open while playing with my belly button as i think about you.

i feel like sex...
i feel like running my tongue across my lips in a crowded room,
oblivious of the numerous physical intruders as i think about you.

i feel like sex...
i feel like stretching out on my bare wood floor and deeply inhaling
the scent of the black love incense that is burning as i think about you.

i feel like sex...

i feel like...

i feel...

you...

in a tub of warm scented water
as the orgasmic organ strokes me
while i jump up and swivel my hips
and play with my belly button
when i run my tongue across my lips
while smelling the scent of black love.

i feel like sex...
when i think about you.

~ :: ~

bath water

i will gladly have you be the water in my bath.
your fluid enveloping me,
soaking me through the very pores of my skin.
the heat of your steam
causes me to come with sweat -
interfusing with your wetness,
giving libation a whole next meaning.
i submerge myself deeper into your liquid.
you lap hungrily around my ankles,
the caps of my knees,
the swelling of my brown honey coated thighs -
causing the organic fibers of my mons
to dance that under water dance
that mermaids use to execute
so long ago that caused sailors
to dive in tumultuous waters
to their deaths only just for a slim
chance to be one with true ecstasy.
while you baptize my belly
and flood my button with your slickness.
you surround the swelling of my breasts.
my erected nipples are
black cherried mountain peaks
that are about to erupt
like mount vesuvius in naples,
covering your pompeii with my hot molten lava.
i lift my head and begin to pour
your liquefied soul over my countenance,
through the strands of my hair,
down my arched back,
to the edge of my backside.
i feel your watery fingertips
trace the length of my person
and slip back into the completeness of yourself
as you continue to embrace my bodily essence.
yes, baby.
i will gladly have you be the water in my bath.
each time we meet, it is always
under the influence of
scented candles, burning frankincense
and the steam rising
from the body of your water.
it places me under your spell
as i willingly submit to your
potent viril cleansing touch.
i will cherish your every drop.

~ :: ~

nudity I

divested of cloth constraints
skin to breathe with nary a restraint
to relax and feel free once again
damp from shower, sprawled happily upon my bed.

~ :: ~

nudity II

I lay bare the extent of my soul
before you,
to eradicate any pretenses between
you and I.
will you do the same for I?
it should only be natural that you
would want to.

~ :: ~

brown canvas

slip of the tongue
as my tongue, being a
paintbrush d`erotique,
slips slides over
your brown canvas -
painting portraits
of salivatic love
giving conception to images
so surreal that
you hold your breath
in wonderment,
afraid the visual would
fade away to
myth and legend.
i take in your
masculine beauty -
imperfect yet perfect...
such an ideal subject
to capture on your
brown canvas.
as i paint your portrait
upon your belly
and around your button,
tracing signs of infinity
down to the edge
of the black forest that is
north of your manhood,
i feel multiple ripples
as they emerge and
finally subside into
gentle shudders
and i realized
that it was
not only you -

but i as well
perceiving the awareness
of our minds,
our bodies and our souls -
entwined and harmonized,
synthesized and synchronized,
creating rhythmical
sounds that can only
be oralized by
the heat of our breath,
the depth of our moans,
the pleasure of our sighs...
so we lay there -
your fingers lost
within my braided locks
satisfied with
your portrait.
and i, cheek on your
brown canvas
and arms wrapped
around your person
holding treasured art,
knowing that we
will work together
again and again -
taking turns
at being artist
and subject
with tongue being
paintbrush d`erotique
slip sliding over
brown canvas
painting portraits
of salivatic love.

~ :: ~

hot candle wax

our yearning is akin to hot candle wax.
as the entrancement of sexuality swelters
and we liquefy and trickle ever so smoothly,
gathering into a reservoir of anointed lubrication,
our bed becomes our candle holder of our passion serum.
we writhe in ecstasy, interfusing freely
as we endure to simmer and dissolve together
becoming and coming into each other
an easy flow of electro-lit jism.

~ :: ~

nectar

i tasted myself on your tongue,
around your mouth,
and down your chin
i smelled myself on the
bridge of your nose
and now i see why
you like to choke
between my thighs
the smell sweet,
the taste like nectar
i would go down on myself...
if i could...
just to flick a lick
at the spring of creation and life
for my own rejuvenation and renewal

~ :: ~

how many ways
can you flip the suckin
lip lockin
with tongues battlin
for more than 69 pole positions
transition fadin from sexin to lovin
right back to fuckin
it's all connected
360 degrees of
mechanisms clickin
fleshy gears shiftin
friction skin to skin and
redefinin concepts of sins
...as myths...
because we be legends
up in this mix
all up in each others joint
gettin this fix
tappin veins...
when dick hit clit
our names become curses
on our eager lips
with teeth gritted
hips smack
sweat rollin black
makin tracks
down backs
floodin ass cracks
annointin our souls

in redemption songs
that seeps so deep
that our spirits weep
for the pleasure beyond
mere comprehension
did i mention the tension?
rigid and wet
stainin sheets with
soaked silhouettes
body parts imprinted
like personal signatures
of love and lust
with a hint of thrust
silken sand dunes shaped
from clutched fingers
graspin and grabbin
as the cummin lingers
with smells and saturation

of *pussification*
thus is the culmination
of our vocation
all this done
in the depth
of one universal breath
and primal screams
finally subside into hushed moans
our minds systematically blown
and the warmth spreads throughout
as we at last lay prone...

~ :: ~

spoken in tongues...

sweet
succulent
rigid
encased with
smooth mocha velvet
lips wrapped
making wet dreams
reality
and secrets exposed
elemental mental
mumblings and rumblings
bubbling to the top of your throat
with sighs
released pressure
long overdue
the pull and the suck
makes hips buck
as you fight tween
holding on for dear life
and letting go
tongue play touche
with your flesh-rod
eyes doing
dice rolls
to the back
of your head
i was compelled
to push you over
the edge
your pleasure
grants me pleasure
that guilty treasure
without any measure
eyes meet
whispers speak
juices secrete
harmonious aromas
further wetting appetites
adding to insatiable cravings
when will the momentum
ever cease?
even with release
there is no
guarantee
that we will ever
be done...

~ :: ~

how ur words
affect
infect
and re-affect
leavin afta affects
of soul shocks
stirrin techtonic plates
up in my erogenous
cranium spots
got my whole bein hot
beyond what kelvin can measure
with no shame at all
we express our treasures
there is that heat
when we meet
bodies clashin like titans
cept there's no defeat
jus wanton abandon
beyond all reason
our sex is sex 4 all seasons
spring 2 be sprung
summer 4 luv's song
fall is passion's fill
and winter jus 2 chill
...together
all u would have 2 do
is speak ur words
declare ur ideas
manifest ur thoughts...
be it whispers
or screams
or cusses thru gritted teeth

and i am there
riding u
the soft confection that i am
whose flava wraps deliciously
around the wet muscle
of ur tongue
seepin gently
in2 ur taste buds
lick by deliberate lick
satisfyin 2 savor
no empty calories
jus complete fulfillment
while u feel me
gradual
persistent
moist
swizzles on ur tip
amid soft glowin moans and
crashin pelvis and ardent hips
twix queen and king
and the crowning of cummin
til those drum beats subside
to the softest of thrummin
thru this sexual osmosis
we absorb each other's
expressions
inspirations
reflections
and there lies the real blessins
so u must kno
how ur words
affect me

~ :: ~

all of this ~ memoir

Brushing teeth was not an option after going down on you. The desire to keep your taste in my mouth won out over fresh breath. As far as I'm concern, my mouth already got a scrub down – all around, in & out – all about.

The thought of tasting you again makes me forget about my previous inhibitions. Sexually cannibalistic - I want to eat you as often as I can without losing sight of who I am. I want to serve you up like you do me, tie on his and her matching bibs, open wide and never waste a drop... Cumming breakfast, lunch and dinner (with some snacks in between), breaking only to take deep breaths or to cat nap in order to rest up.

You got me open enough to receive and give with little worry about tomorrow. And when all is said and done over and over again, I find myself missing your presence the moment you leave my sight to go into the subway station to head for home. It was a good weekend.

So I appreciate this feeling because it is genuine and it is ours. And even though we've shared physical intimacy before, this road that we're traveling is new and unpaved. Where we were then is not where we are now because both our intentions are on some other level. There is still the extreme sexual attraction. There is still the jokes and laughter. But now there are conversations and sharing and not forgetting who we are as individuals.

And the beauty of it all is that you understand when I tell you that I want to take it one day at a time. You say for me to take my time, you ain't going no where and that makes me feel just fine.

This is new, again. I feel good, again. And it feels fun, again. And I want to feel safe, again. Safe enough to go down on you, knowing you appreciate and moan with every lick, suck and nip. Especially when my mind plays back your face between my thighs eating me out like Grandma's Sunday night dinner. I am so determined to bring you on the brink of madness and drop you ever so gingerly over the edge as you have done so to me many times before.

All of this...
...all of this is why I don't brush my teeth after going down on you.

verse 9

-::-

heart

it takes a lot of heart to not only survive through generations of racism, but to thrive and prosper despite the bullshit. let's not fool ourselves. it is what it is. humans packed and shipped for profit. conditioned and brainwashed into "believing" that as a collective, we are "less than"...

but through it all we have persevered and our scars along the way are nothing less than badges of honor and respect that supersedes the lies that were force fed to us beautiful people of african ancestry. we still may have a long way to go, but in spite of everything, we continue to move forward... making strides in the right direction while hurdling challenges. we be doing our damn thang!

until you lived it,
you will never understand it.

~ :: ~

run

i run...
cuz have no choice.
i hear the beat
of the antagonist's drums.
they're after me again.
so again, i run...
i run...
i run so hard
that i can hear
the constant beat of rhythms
bein created
by my broad, ebon feet
poundin out a rebellious reply
to their persistent thrummin.
where their sounds
are carried away by the
fleetin elemental winds,
my sound
is carried through the
nurturin belly of the earth.
i maneuver tween trees
to avoid gettin yoked
by low swingin vines.
my breath pumps out hot
like a hot steam engine.
it is the only tell tale sign
of how hard i have to run.
so again, i run...
i run...
i run so hard
to avoid the hunters
that want to take
that which i was born wit.
it is mine,
this coveted prize!
and i will not rest
until i am free from
my pursuers.
my heart is heavy but strong
my chest pounds wit rage
my eyes attempt to go
unfocused.
i am tired.

but i refuse to stop.
i refuse to give up.
my goal is finally
within my sight:
a mountain, proud and strong,
nearly as aged as the creator,
beckonin me wit sweet
promises of victory
sayin, "salvation! salvation!"
so again, i run...
i run...
i run so hard
as my blood rushes through
my body like a tidal wave
and ignites me like fire
takin me higher and higher
to the promised land
where black rocks
on mountain tops
will shelter me from my
sworn enemies
and i will be triumphant
in my struggle to survive!
so i remain focused,
blockin out
discordant drums and
shriekin horns
that are used to try
to distract me from my goal,
that are used to try
to keep my hopes from risin,
that are used to try
to wear down my spirit's flame.
and i turned inward to
concentrate upon the song
that is orchestrated within
my bein,
usin consistent rhythms
created by broad, ebon feet:
as the underlinin beat to my zen.
a break in the trees.
a clearin.
the base of my salvation!

i push harder.
so again, i run...
i run...
i run so hard
as i smell the hints
of fresh mountain air,
caressin me wit sweet
promises of hope
sayin, "you are almost there!
do not give up!"
i hadn't realized until now
of how much i had to give
for this cause!
thoughts of bein captured
were overshadowed by
the want of bein free.
despite the fact that i can still
vaguely hear them
closin in on me.
loomin closer and closer...
black rocks
on mountaintops!
loomin closer and closer...
black rocks
on mountaintops!
loomin closer and closer...
black rock
on mountaintops!
i feel them snappin at my heels...
can't stop
can't give up
it is my birthright!
i leap
and my broad, ebon feet
strikes black rocks,
sparks flyin out as a testimony
of my defiance
to my pursuin enemies
as i bolt up to the heights of
salvation!
i look down at them
flounderin in confusion,
their horses refusin

the steep climb.
one even cursed me
as he cracked
his whip at me in anger.
i denied him the chance
to divest me of my birthright,
which shielded me from
the heat of the day and
the coolness on the night.
i denied him the chance
to sell to strangers
in the market
the strands of my bein,
spreadin pieces of me
all over this creation –
for a profit
that i, myself,
will never see
or could never claim
it rightfully mine,
in their society.
i watched them calmly,
takin in their frustration.
and i smiled
only
as an
african
can...
~ :: ~

133

the pope

a dichotomy.
the pope.
[flip the coin]
the grand dragon.
demon twins begot by evil.
a dry birth.
one subtle,
the other obvious -
both underhanded.
both sent to accomplish
the same goal.
the catholic church
used religion to enslave,
the ku klux klan
uses religion to purge
all in the name of God...
but isn't lucifer a god?
the god of hell?
chaotic chaos swirling
like a hurricane mix.
it's like burning the candle
at both ends.
that is...to cover more ground.
the pope gets us into america,
the grand dragon takes us out
of america:
slavery.
death.
slavery and death both justified
by a twisted religion.
the same twisted religion
that is twined like the rope
that hangs my brothers & sisters
until they choke with the
eternal darkness of slumber.
as the pope and
the grand dragon
skip merrily down the road,
they hum the hymns and anthems
of
Oppressors, Dictators
and other various Madmen
that shamelessly commit

their heinous crimes
in the name of the
Almighty...
or is it:
in the name of their almighty?
the pope.
the grand dragon.
they were spotted
the other day
shopping in the same
clothing store
[bennetton? saks?
macy's? bargain hunters?]
seems like white sheets
and tall white caps
are the fashion
for the next few centuries
for the white skin.
it's believed to be
where that term
"white sale" came from:
the whites sail across the sea
and pluck us like ripe fruits.
the whites sell my ancestors
like cattle in the market.
and the dollars were use
to lace the pope's robes
and to fashion
gold encrusted crosses
until our productive commodity
ran out
then the grand dragon
raised his burning cross and
proclaimed his purpose in
america:
to purge america
of the BLACKNESS
of the DARKNESS
of the SHAME
of the GUILT
"Blind Denial In The Name
Of Self Righteousness"
was the Gospel they lived by

and they were out to get
not only Africans,
but
Native Americans
Asians
Polynesians
Indigenous Australians
Indians - from India
- people with hues
and various tones of Melanin.
like a world rainbow ice cream
and they wanted to have a lick.
they had the fever
for the flavor.
the flavor of
oil,
gold,
gems,
trees,
animal skins...
every natural resource
on this earth.
and instead of taking
what was needed,
everything just got TOOK.
a global sham!
the ultimate flim flam!
damn!
the pope gave sanctions
to these explorers & expeditioners
to these rapists &
pillagers
and payment to his "holiness"
in return -
to line his crypt...
[oops! excuse me! i mean...]
the vatican
with the Holy treasures
that belonged to the world.
that's what happens when
one with no Spirit
seek to capture everyone else's.
the pope.

the grand dragon.
a dragon is a serpent with legs.
when the serpent
pissed God off
he was cursed to crawl
on his belly for all eternity:
a snake.
the word "grand": big, huge.
so when one calls himself:
"Grand Dragon",
he is in turn calling himself:
"A great, big snake"...
in the grass.
the only masked coward.
the pope.
the grand dragon.
slavery.
death.
thief.
murderer.
demon twins.
[flip the coin]

~ •• ~

tell me

Come and sit with me for a while under the old oak tree
And tell me of my ancestors while we feel the warm summer breeze.
Tell me of my home and the land from which I came.
Tell me of my people and let me know my true name.

As we hold hands and walk through the cane fields,
You will tell me of the wonderments that my ancestors have built:
The villages, the cities, the pyramids, and the charting of the stars.
The true worship of the Creator, the society and the travel of near and far.

When we sit out under the stars in the coolness of the night,
You could tell me of my people and their strength of might.
Of the wars that took place between tribe and tribe.
And together we can count the souls of the warriors that have died.

We climb the baobab tree and cut monkey bread from a branch
And speak of the multitude the oppressors had set out to catch.
Let me know of how my people even sold each other;
Men and women, old and young, sister and brother.

As we walk along the shores and watch the sun go down,
We can talk about how my people held their ground.
The ones that fought the devils that came to rape the land,
As they stoically did battle down to the very last man.

While we cross the expanse of the mighty and massive waters,
Speak to me about slave ships and their soulless operators,
Of how they packed my people as if they were pieces of rotted meat,
And brought us all to a land made putrid with lies and deceit.

As the sun warms our backs from the heat of the mid-day,
Talk to me about the lucrative business of the slave trade.
How they destroyed whole families and broke my people's spirit
And how we were forced to bear the pain of the white man's whip.

We dig for yams and bake them in the ground on red hot stones
While talking about how my people were taken from their homes.
To North America, South America, Haiti, Trinidad, Tobago,
Barbados, England, Jamaica, Cuba and Puerto Rico.

Let us converse freely as we sit and warm ourselves by the fire
About my people and the freedom that they truly desired.
Tell me about the rebellions, the revolutions and the runaways,
The successes, the failures and the prices that we all have had to pay.

As we snap green beans on the front porch in the mid-afternoon,
You will tell me about my people's ability to survive and bloom.
About our collective genius that shows in our accomplishments
And how we have a true ability to create with beauty and excellence.

We listen to the night rhythms of the crickets and of the cicadas
And discuss the deepness of the magnificence in which God has made us
From the beauty of our soul to our various shades of brown.
From the strength of our spirit to the many ways we wear our textured crowns.

We talk and till the soil, planting for the spring, to harvest in the fall
And as we talk there is music that sends out to us that ancient call,
You say, "Shhh! Doya hear those drums in Mother Earth, rhythm deep?
Do we love each other, do we dance or do we fight our enemies to the beat?
Do we pray, do we live or do we make love in its wake?
Do we nurture, do we grow or do we put back what we take?
Tell me, my child what is it that you hear for once and for all?
Now it is your turn to tell me what you hear when the ancient drum calls."

~ :: ~

137

instrumental purpose

our minds are the instruments of the spirit
which endows us with perseverance and gives us great merit.
our purpose in life no longer overcast nor worn out
as we continue to live on without any doubt.

our eyes are the instruments of vision,
to acknowledge past, present and future perception.
our eyes are the jeweled orbs that will record history
for all our descendants to learn from for infinity.

our ears are the instruments of balance,
speed, agility and gracefulness of dance
that helps heighten our reflexes in times of need
and warns us of dangers in time to heed.

our voices are the instruments of power
that will make our enemies forever cower
at the strength and convictions of our words
and for all eternity we will be heard.

our hands are the instruments of war,
the formed fist will destroy that which will shackles us no more.
our hands will forge that unyielding red hot iron-steel
as the promise of our enemies' demise is made real.

our feet are the instruments of flight
to survey the world through travel and sight.
to bear witness to new and different places
and to understand and respect those of other races.

our bodies are the instruments of the sacred temple,
blessed by the Creator, our function is simple:
seek the oneness of all and acquire true wealth
through our and our children's prosperity and good health.

~ :: ~

dance of the sun children

there was a time
when we were free.
not so much
as being carefree,
but still we were freeborn.
so we rejoiced .
always shall we rejoice in life.

there was a time
when we were enslaved.
not so much
as being annihilated,
but still we were shackled.
so we persevered.
always shall we persevere in life

there was a time
when we were rebellious.
not so much
as being cold-blooded,
but still we were warriors.
so we fought.
always shall we fight in life

there was a time
when we were "emancipated".
not so much
as being freed,
but still we were oppressed.
so we liberated ourselves.
always shall we be liberated in life

there was a time
when we were driven.
not so much
as being obsessed,
but still we were focused.
so we progressed.
always shall we progress in life

there was a time
when we were profound.
not so much
as being all-knowing,
but still we were aware.
so we reflected.
always shall we reflect in life.

there was a time
when we were heavenly.
not so much
as being self-righteous,
but still we were spiritual.
so we aspired.
always shall we aspire in life.

there was a time
when we were love
not so much
as being desire,
but still we were harmony.
so we were one.
always shall we be one in life.

we, the sun children dance
a rejoiceful dance
a persevering dance
a warriors' dance
a liberating dance
a progressive dance
a reflective dance
an aspiring dance
a unifying dance

we dance to the heartbeat
of our mother earth
as our father creator
smiles his fondness upon us
like the rays of the sun.

we the sun children, dance the dance of
brass, bronze, brown, chocolate, cinnamon, ebony, ecru, ochre, mahogany,
maroon, red-brown, sepia, tan, tawny, yellow - the blessed rainbow.

we the sun children, dance the dance of
africa, north american, south america, canada, the caribbean, europe, asia - the diaspora.

we the sun children dance the dance of
rejoice, perseverance, rebellion, liberation, progression, wisdom, spirituality, love –
the life.

our seeds spread far and wide, becoming beautiful hued gardens
that flourish never-ending.

~ :: ~

the anticipated death

shuffle off this mortal coil
to take one's last sleep.
cross the stygian ferry
to go out like the snuff of a candle.
come to an untimely end,
catching one's death.
kicking the bucket.
hopping the twig.
turning up one's toes.
stone dead.
mutton.
that last gasp.
and with one foot in the grave,
the final race is ran.
corpse
carcass
bones
skeletal remains
dry bones
defunct
dust
ashes
carrion

racism

~:~

thru the penis canal

Yo mama must of done somethin to piss you off.

I see the anger smolderin in your dark demon orbs as you saunter down the hallway, talkin to only those that carry the legendary 3rd leg, surroundin yourself in the office w/ those that carry the apple of Adam, while wearin pale skin.

I believe that the only reason you got married was to oppress your wife.

Much like how you're tryin to oppress the levels of estrogen in your dept.

Much like how you set out to remove the growth of the Black Lotus from your sight. Did we scare you?

When you saw the 3 of us together, did we remind you of your mama?

Was she brown like we?

I bet the reason why you're so bitter cuz you resent the blood that flows thru your veins.

I bet you felt resentment cuz every time you looked in the mirror, YOU saw hair so tightly curled that it threatened to make you Black like me & she & she:

The Black Lotus.

When you see us, you see the reality.

I believe you saw as your forefathers raped my foremothers each time you looked into that mirror.

And instead of admittin to yourself the evil of the actions of your ancestors, you secretly blamed us:

The Black Lotus cuz we were tangible & lively & strong.

While your predecessors were untouchable & dead & weak.

So you systematically set out to destroy our bond, demon-boy.

("No lunch in her office on Fridays w/ her friends anymore!")

("WHY is she hangin out in our dept.?! Doesn't she have enough work to do?!")

However, our bond was strong & spiritually impervious to space & time (plus we had e-mail).

The collective we cannot be destroyed by the petty fears of weak minded pale skins that carry the 3rd leg & swear that they have been birthed thru the penis canal instead of the vaginal canal.

At 1st, the Black Lotus was angry.

But as we looked thru you, past your skin & into your soul, we saw your weakness.

The weakness that you tried to hide in layers & layers of coldness & indifference.

&

We found you wantin.

We found you lackin.

We found you helpless.

We found you...power - less.

Yo mama must have definitely pissed you off cuz you realized that you were birthed thru a vaginal canal & not a penis canal & you can't stand the fact that your forefather couldn't control his demon lusts when he subjugated my foremother.

cuz every time you see us – the Black Lotus & our lovely locks & braids, it reminds you of your hair: the only tell tale sign of the true state of your genes.

That's why you tried to banish us from your sight cuz you can't stand to face the truth.

But in the end, enlightenment will come to all & you will either stand firm & bask in the truth, or you will cower like a mangy dog in the shame.

But regardless, the Black Lotus will continue to strive.

So continue to suppress the estrogen in your dept.

So continue to try to suppress the Black Lotus.

So continue to surround yourself w/ pale male penises.

So keep doin' it.

But remember this: each & every time you look 'n2 a mirror, you see the only person that you truly hate - yourself.

~ :: ~

subversive subway revolt

so the earth stood
stock still
underground
cuz 4
3 days
those iron horses
were corralled...

just as his namesake,
toussaint fought
4 his people's rights
2 be able 2 afford
2 live/work/die in nyc

so the earth stood
stock still
underground
while above ground
we found
other ways
2 make our
appointed rounds...
like walking across bridges
while bloomtaki
tried 2 snow us all
with bullying propaganda
on crisp, clear, sunny days.

the beast wished us angry
at the man who "inconvenienced"
us new yorkers...

this same man
who was fighting
2 bring some
convenience
2 his own co-workers.

the beast wanted 2
scapegoat him
cock block his efforts
deny him martydom
2 no avail
toussaint was seen
recognize as a voice
an advocate

and no media slant
could stop
what we all witnessed
wit the collective
first eye

yes...

so the earth stood
stock still
underground
and his voice
and their voices
were heard
2 the rhythm of
multipeds trekking
across concrete and steel connections
just making it
2 the other side

ain't that like all of
life's challenges?
2 make it 2 the otha side...
take a breath...
with back unbent...
and head up?

recognize that
2 execute change
sometimes
you have 2 say,

"fuck it!
pull dat switch, baby!
make the earth stand
stock still
underground!"

and hold
a whole
gotdamn city hostage
just 2 be taken
seriously....

-:: -

politics/pawns/political prisoners

you know...
i'm not a political person.
i never was.
politics never interest me
and maybe that's cuz i see things
in more simpler terms.
"politics" is defined as the science of government.
"government" is defined as a body of persons authorized to govern.
"govern" is defined as to guide, control and determine.
as well "govern" comes from the greek word "kyberman"
which means "to steer".
ultimate translation: politics = MANIPULATION.
in essence, politics is nothing more or less than
a massive tree pissing contest...
marking boundaries and territories...
the elite few who's running shit by manipulating
the multitudes of the common woman and man.
using their lives as fodder for an intricate chess game.
pawns and, if need be, scapegoats to take the fall
or to be made examples of in an elaborate effort
to cow the masses into various forms of submission
so folk will be too damned discouraged
to think outside "the box" or
too damned discouraged to fight for their human AND civil rights.
guiding, controlling, determining the fate of mumia.
blatantly ignoring facts and truths.
questioning NOT the inconsistencies simply because
an example needs to be made.
a sacrificial lamb, if you will.
like a bad acid tripping flashback of when "massa"
would break a "slave's" spirit by stringing him up
in front of all his family
to crack that whip across his melanated flesh
until the skin broke and the blood would well up and
begin to drain, not only his life fluid...
but his fighting spirit as well.
this is how i view politics.
it's just an evolved form of slavery where
people like
mumia abu jamal
leonard peltier
assata shakur
shaquanda cotton
and yes - all of YOU
...WE...

145

...are all in this position of being manipulated
into being forcibly restrained at this government's merest whims
thus becoming political prisoners.
to guide -- your fate...
to control -- your fate...
to determine -- your fate...
knowing this, however, does not mean we walk with
a defeatist attitude.
being aware makes us a stronger, more unified people
who will not be lulled into a false state of security.
we keep our eyes open, our ear to the ground and our voices loud.
information is a powerful tool to turn the tides.
so when we say, "free mumia!",
we are saying to free ourselves.
so when we fight to save this man's life,
we are fighting to save our lives.
persistence and perseverance is essential
to keep that momentum going.
like i said before,
i'm not a political person...
never was.
politics never interest me
and that's cuz i do see things
in more simpler terms.
it is what it is
and we must do
what needs
to be
done.
~ :: ~

verse 10

~ :: ~

the bonus round

levity n. 1. lack of seriousness; frivolty. 2. lightness

satire n. the use of irony, ridicule, etc., in writing.

burlesque n. 1. an imitation of a literary or dramatic work for comic effect; a parody. 2. a theatrical entertainment characterized by coarse comedy.

that all being said... enjoy...

chuckle

the impact of my grill

you hop your punk ass out in front of me,
choosing to be heedless of my speed.
all you see is an old, well used, tired van
and in your mind, you think, "i know i can..."
so just like sex, you hit the gas,
in that little car made out of fiberglass.
and here i am, in my two tons of steel,
a determined, angry bitch behind the wheel.
i slams on my brakes, cussin' and swearin'.
your fiberglass alls my grill's gonna be wearin'.
Damn! Shit! Dumbass! Punk muthafucka!!
with tweezers they'll pick yo' ass from my bumper!
what was on your mind? where was your brains?
"oh yessss.... now i see..."i think with disdain.
there she sat in the seat, wind blowing her hair,
influencing mr. hormone man to do a dare.
he feels like a man now, his dick cock-diesel.
but he's no more to me than a limp ass weasel.
visions, i had, of ramming his car,
the impact of my grill with intent to mar.
him through the windshield, a boneless husk
and barbie through the glass, flying into the dusk
and ME behind the wheel, my van now still,
knowing they cannot survive the impact of my grill.

~ :: ~

a mad maniacal mutant roach on roller blades smokin' blunts an' takin' mu-fuckas out

I'm a mad roach, baby.
I'm a mad maniacal mutant roach.
I'm a mad maniacal mutant roach on roller blades, smokin blunts & takin mu-fuckas out.
Ya can't take me, ya punk sucka!
I'm big! I'm large!
At least 3 or 4 inches strong!
& I ain't afraid of ya ass.
Ya can stare me down all ya want.
I stares back atcha while puffin on my Philly blunt.
[This puffs for you, baby!]
I do shots of Raid up my nasal track just for kicks!
Shee-it!
Cuz I'm a mad maniacal mutant roach on roller blades, smokin blunts & takin mu-fuckas out.

Yeah, I lives on the edge.
Shee-it... I skates on the edge wit my roller blades.
I can dodge ya ass while skatin backwards & rollin up a blunt at the same time.
I don't spill a seed, bitch!
Cuz I'm bad.
I ain't got no past, no future.
Just livin for the here & now.
I'm here.
I'm now
I'm into survivin.
It's all about me.
What?
Step on me?!
Is ya crazy?!
Baby, are ya shoes big enough?
Ya better get me on the first try,
cuz if you don't,
I'll be up the wall laughin atcha dumb ass
& blowin smoke in ya face.
Cuz I'm a mad maniacal mutant roach on roller blades smokin blunts & takin mu-fuckas out.

I'm in ya fridge while you snoozin,
Eatin up ya hero sammiches,
Piggin out on ya Haagen Daas Ice Cream,
& chuggin down ya 40 oh-zees.
Shee-it! Them blunts make ya hungry after awhile.
I gotta do what I gotta do.
I gots ta get mine.
Then I sits on your couch,
Light up another blunt & chill while watchin your cable t.v., the playboy channel,
bitch!
Ain't nuthin but a thang, baby.
Cuz I'm a mad maniacal mutant roach on roller blades smokin blunts & takin mu-
fuckas out.

I saw ya woman the otha day, punk.
You know that heifa try to turn her nose up at me?
I only paid her a compliment.
I said,
"Hey mama!
Don't you know a white woman's mini-skirt cain't fit a black woman's ass?
All I sees from this low vantage point is 2 full brown moons in risin!
What's ya sign, sweetness?"
& she tried to step on me! Me - the Mad Maniacal!
But I did a backflip & a 180° spin & skated from unda dat broad's boot.
Then I threw up the peace sign - I gives her the middle.
& told that double moon risin heifa to kiss my cucarachan ass!
I blew a puff of herb in her face.
Who da hell do she think she is?
Cuz I'm a mad maniacal mutant roach on roller blades smokin' blunts an' takin' mu-
fuckas out.

So I want to leave ya wit a little word from the Mad Maniacal:

Don't you ever fuck wit the roach that's Mad Maniacal,
Smokin' Philly blunts & actin quite hysterical.
The next time ya come at me wit you little ass shoe,
I'll shove it up ya ass & make you go, "Boo! Hoo!"
& the next time ya bitch try to pass me by,
I'm gonna get up in her face & spit in her eye.
Cuz I'm THE Mad Maniacal Mutant Roach on Roller Blades, Smokin' Blunts &
takin Mu-Fuckas out.
You better watch ya back cuz I'll gitcha without a doubt!

~ :: ~

p m s

he tread obliviously
into my mental storm,
not paying heed
to the fall of his feet
and me not trying
to warn off
unsuspecting prey.
his foolish plundering,
because of his
lack of attention,
only made him the sacrifice
that i required to placate
my female ire.
as i snapped him up
like brittle bones,
i grinned the grin
of a predator
with a sated appetite.
yes, he was a hapless victim
that couldn't grasp
the trap falls of my wild
feminine bestiality.
while i consumed
the last of his
consciousness,
his bewildered thoughts
relayed to me
one final question:
"why?"
and as i licked
the last morsel
of his effervescence
from my fingertips
-- a meal well had --
i replied:

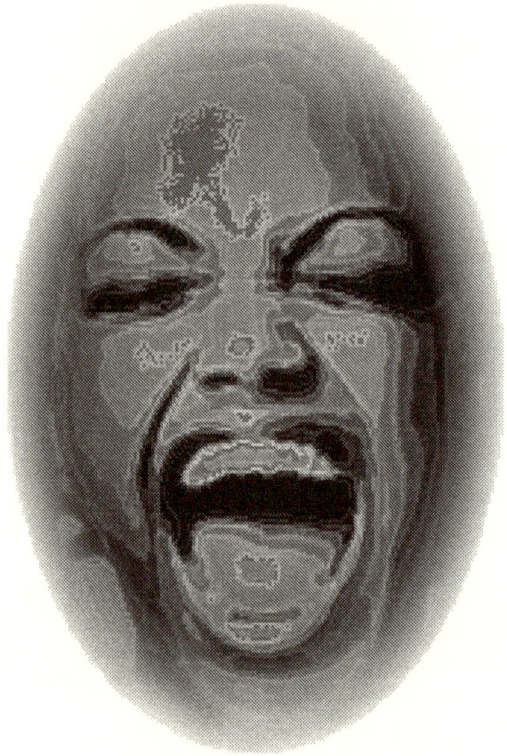

"because, gotdamn it,

you too bit the apple!"

-:-

parable of a bean sprout

i saw a bean sprout
on my friend's red carpet.
a refugee from a box of lo mein,
by way of kum kau's.
just laying there,
spent and twisted – lifeless.
its demise will either be by the
vacuumous maw of the
amazing suck-o-matic
or by a pair of
determined fingertips,
whose command center
demands tidiness.
ironically, the purpose
of the bean sprout's
presence became nil
because that same
entity that governed
those determined fingertips
as well as command
the power of the
amazing suck-o-matic
was also guilty of poor eating habits.
carelessly, he allowed
the bean sprout to become
a victim and fall to its death
through the prongs of a
plastic eating implement.
[such a waste of a good
vegetable in this society!]
no one will ever know
how this beautiful, tender
and edible seedling
of the bean plant family
could have truly contributed
to this same entity's health.
we all will never know.
we can only speculate
on how that one bean sprout
by way of kum kau's
could have made a difference
in the life of the same man
that snuffed out
its very existence.
~ :: ~

culture

It's not your issues that bother me.
It's when you have problems that you need to seek therapy.
You see, you are cheese and I no longer consume your dairy products.
The flava of your culture has very little to do with headwraps, lapas, dashikis,
Black power and Mother Africa.
Your culture flava has to do with germinating actions that lead to viral results.
Reeking infectious havoc, causing those that trust you, only to become your
victims instead.
Just cuz you carry the blessing of melanin, does not negate that you are Gouda
deep down in your soul.
Swiss be your thoughts -- your ideas be squalid.
And when you open your mouth to speak, Limburger is what you squeak.
Cheddar chatterings laced with Provolone promises could do no less than give
great emphasis...
That you are cheesy.
That curdling, shoddy, piss poor existence that you attempt to pass off like some
gargantuan champ.
Cuz you refuse to see yourself as the Gorgonzola clump you really are.
You Muenster!
So, before you cultivate your mold and your curds and your whey, I want you to
understand on this very day:

Little Sister Muffet
Chilled on her tuffet
Scoping your curds and whey
You played like a confider
Til you tried to get inside her
But she caught ya with some anti-mold spray
The blow was rightly dealt
Your funky spores did melt
Little Sister Muffet cheered in delight
Your nonsense was repelled
So she chuckled and she yelled
"Mr. Thing, there'll be no CHEESE tonight"

~ :: ~

for brad

Baby, ya regular.
& I don't mean regular
like bowel movements or colonics,
kaopectate or other tonics.
I mean regular like
pork sammiches & red wine -
fallin asleep on someone's futon in no time,
wit drivel escapin ya cavernous maw,
stainin the pillow. Yep, we all saw!
But we LUVS ya, Baby --
cuz ya regular.

Ya regular like
Black folks & ol' niggas.
Don't look at me like "How you figure?!"
Ya blow up the spot wit ya brimstone & fire.
Ya stuff be sooo good, it's off the wire.
But when ya finally exit that stage pulpit,
ya start committin some outrageous shit!...
But we LUVS ya, Baby --
cuz ya regular.

Ya regular like
constant hunger like a mufuck!
Willin to confiscate ya best friend's last bit o' potluck!
Ya damn sure ain't no hunter nor a gatherer.
Ya jus a stone cold unmitigated food snatcha.
Boy, we coulda all just almost sworn
that ya were carrying that dreaded tapeworm!
I ain't neva seen an appetite so damn RAVENOUS!
Makes me wanna jus plain ol cuss!
But we LUVS ya, Baby --
cuz ya regular.

Ya regular like
actin like ya don't need nary a lick o' sleep.
Up all hours, day & night, dancin on ya feet.
Screamin & hollerin like a damn lunatic!
Cain't help yaself. Ya need ya house music fix.
Yellin at the d.j.'s, strippin off all ya clothes...
Pushin yaself til you fall out, half comatose.
Once a dancin warrior, now passed out on the floor,
Half naked & sweatin as ya begin to snore.
But we LUVS ya, Baby --
cuz ya regular.

Ya regular like
Comin to someone else's house wit ya dirty laundry.
Sleepin on somebody's floor like a Brooklynite refugee.
Boisterous cacklin that leaves ya in stitches.
Lord! I ain't neva heard a man's voice reach so many pitches!
Creatin ya own languages & patterns of speeches too:
"Shemdalah, scoobie, & sceebie..." Whachoo sayin, Boo?
But we LUVS ya, Baby --
cuz you regular.
And if ya tweren't regular,
ya wouldn't be the Brad
that we all know
and love.

~ :: ~

to thy breasts be true!

A silicone breast by any other name still leaks the same...
-Shelley Jefferson

Neither silicone, nor padded be, but to thyself be true and au naturale...
- Vilma Alvarez

To pad or not to pad...
This is the question.
Whether 'tis nobler only in thy mind
to suffer the underwires and biting straps of outrageous brassieres.
And by burning thy offending garment, to free thy breasts?
To sag; to droop...
Forever more!
And by drooping...to say we end the heartache
and the thousand unnatural welts upon shoulder and back that our tender, supple flesh is
forcibly heir to.
'Tis a consummation devoutly to be wished.
To sag; to droop...
To droop perchance to be free: ay, there's the rub.
For in thy freedom of thy breasts what dreams may come when we have shrugged off this
man-made bondage.
We must not give pause:
it is our cowardice to act that make challenges of so long life.
For who should bear thy straps
and buckles of thy bra – man's bondage fantasy;
lifting and separating our mounds of pure joy;
spurning the love of our natural bodies
for sake of a desired contour made in demand by society –
falsies, wonder-bras, corsets, silicone and the bloody like;
for a man's conditioned love, thus his compromising touch.
Let us bare a dagger and cut away this overbearing burden.
No longer will we grunt and sweat to bind our breasts,
which is the dread of this life.
Tied up and bound for sake of man's vanity?
Tied up and bound because he cannot control his bestial lusts?
Thus we tie and bind our femininity and our strength?
Nay, I say!
No more shall we be cowed by the masculine overdrive.
Sisters!
Free thy breasts!
Let them be breath!
Allow them to sway happily in the wind!
No more welts!
No more cut flesh!
No more strap burns!
Sever the ties that bind and be free!!!
THIS IS ANARCHY!!!

-:-

the fly

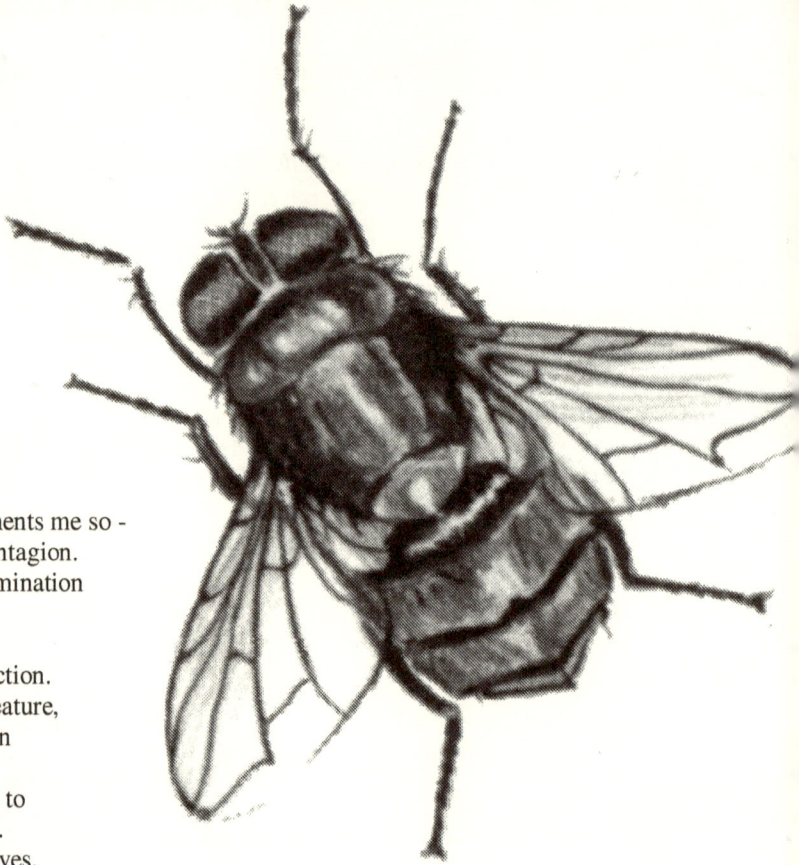

the fly, she torments me so -
conductor of contagion.
infestation, abomination
and mephitic.
i recoil at her
sexpediculed taction.
a diminutive creature,
the consideration
of her existence
renders my skin to
creep and crawl.
i break out in hives.
she skeeves me so.

~ :: ~

hamhocks 'n gams

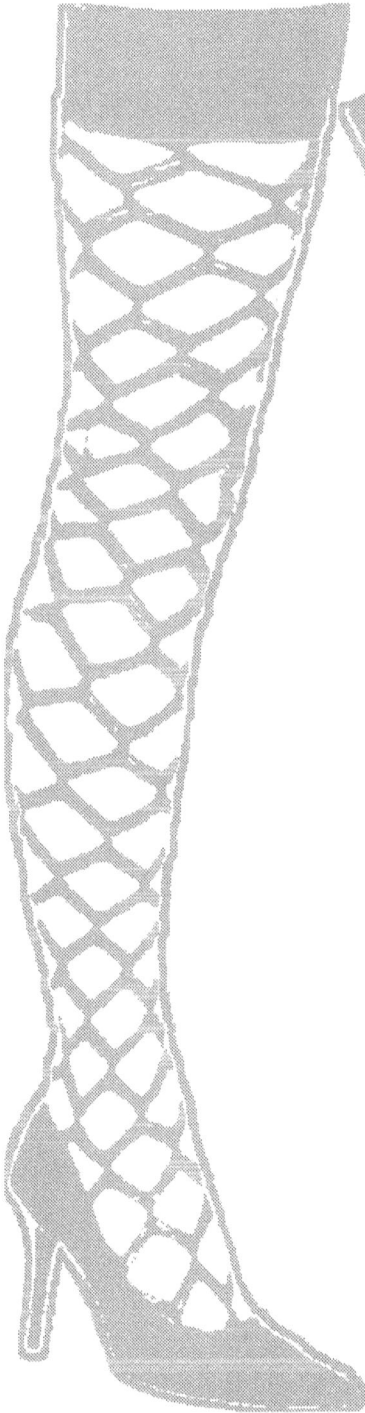

His mama's hamhocks had
nuthin on her gams.
Jus enuf meat & muscle
to make him wrestle...
wit thoughts of cravin hunger.
Suppressed appetite
became expanded
when his eyes panned
& focused on her fleshed out gams.
His mind screamed "DAMN IT! "
But his mouth whistle
an even higher pitch of appreciation...
It was more so to keep the drool
from drippin at the corners of his
mouth & makin him look like
the voracious
brute he really was.
It was all he could do cuz...
His mama's hamhocks had
nuthin on her gams.
He wouldn't even tell his best man.
Oh hell not.
Then he'd too would want some from her pot
of goody-goodies.
Havin men tryin to beat down their woodies
as she passed them by.
Legs as thick as beef stew
and as shapely as sculpted sinew...
Men would jump up to pay their dues
just to have her walk on their backs.
Masculine meltdown into wussies.
They can't even survive the glimpse of her legs,
let allow her pussy.
But they say bravery and stupidity
goes hand in hand.
And my God! He wanted to taste those gams!
So in a short synapse of time
he plotted within his mind
of how he can get down wit that dime - piece.
cuz a piece was all he wanted to get...
Just to stick in & get it a lil wet...
Just a lil taste of....
If he can just get the taste of...
Just a lil taste of ...
If he can just get the taste of...
them gams!

her entourage

Blueberry stained lips
Stained his primal mind
As his panoramic view
Suddenly became narrow
Upon her naturally grand entrance.

Coconut drenched fingertip
Is what he violently envisioned
Tracing barometric patterns
And turbulent hurricane swirls
Along the strong and weak of his back.

Swurvy-curvy mango hips
Hypnotized his once frantic thoughts
With promises of being swooned, swayed
And wrapped in the swelling seas
Of her funky femme fatale.

Brandied black cherried nips
He feverishly wished to envelope
To feed hungrily upon
So that her nourishing flavor
Would stain his lips everlasting.

Blueberry stained lips,
Coconut drenched fingertips,
Swurvy-curvy mango hips and
Brandied black cherried nips
Were her entourage...

And he desperately fiended to be down...

And in their wake he wanted to drown...

But upon his emergence from daydream...

She was no longer around.

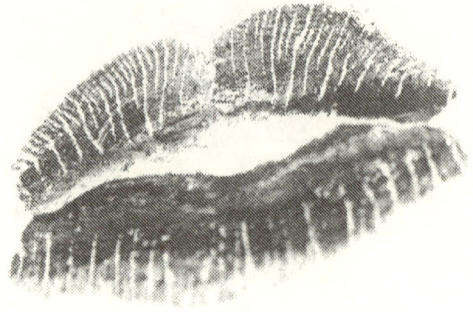

~ :: ~

* 9 7 8 0 6 1 5 1 5 8 0 2 0 *